KU-488-765

To Mushie
with all my love
Cypa 1966

JOHN KEPLER

JOHN KEBLE.

JOHN KEPLER

ANGUS ARMITAGE

FABER AND FABER
24 Russell Square
London

First published in mcmlxvi
by Faber and Faber Limited
24 Russell Square London WC1
Printed in Great Britain by
Latimer Trend & Co Ltd Plymouth
All rights reserved

© Angus Armitage 1966

PREFACE

More than three hundred years have now elapsed since the untimely death of the great astronomer Johannes Kepler; but the drama of his life's pilgrimage and the historic importance of his scientific achievements have never ceased to awaken the interest and wonder of later ages.

Starting out from the traditional natural philosophy of the sixteenth century, he arrived after years of patient investigation at the fundamental laws of planetary motion and at the conception of forces acting between celestial bodies, thus preparing the way for Newton. Dogged by ill-health, living under the shadow of impending or actual war and persecuted by Catholics and Protestants alike, Kepler brought his work to completion in the face of almost incredible difficulties.

Of universal human interest is the epic story of Kepler's heroic confrontation of a tragic destiny, of his steadfast loyalty to his Faith, of his princely self-giving in adversity. In the setting of European history, he presents himself in his books and letters as a courtier of the eccentric Emperor Rudolph II, as a cross-bench sectary in an age of religious strife, as a waif of the Thirty Years' War.

In tracing Kepler's life-story, I have leaned heavily upon the scholarship of the late Max Caspar's definitive biography of the astronomer, *Johannes Kepler* (Zweite Auflage, Stuttgart,

1950), available also in the English translation of Dr. C. Doris Hellman (London and New York, 1959). I have also read with profit Mr. Arthur Koestler's evocation of Kepler and his age in his book *The Sleepwalkers* (London, 1959). However, in summarizing Kepler's scientific writings, I have taken a fresh look at the original texts themselves, now becoming available in the magnificent Munich edition of the astronomer's collected works and letters, inaugurated in 1938 by Max Caspar and the late Walther von Dyck. I have also consulted Caspar's German translations of works by Kepler. A few other translations and articles of particular interest are cited in the text.

The transition from medieval to modern scientific thought is nowhere better illustrated than in Kepler's writings; and I hope that the book may be of interest to students of the history and philosophy of science no less than to the general reader for whom it is primarily intended and for whose sake I have ventured, in title and text, to anglicize the Christian names of Kepler and his family circle and to refer to his books by the English equivalents of their titles. I have also included a short Glossary of technical terms not explained in the text for the sake of any readers to whom they may be unfamiliar.

Figures 9 and 10 are reproduced from A. Wolf, *A History of Science, Technology and Philosophy in the Sixteenth and Seventeenth Centuries*, Second Edition, London, 1950, by kind permission of the Publishers, Messrs. George Allen and Unwin Ltd.

A. A.

CONTENTS

Preface   *page* 5

1. An Ancient Quest   11
2. Seed-Time   21
3. Tübingen and Graz   26
4. Planetary Problems   31
5. The *Cosmographic Mystery*   41
6. From Graz to Prague   51
7. The Legacy of Tycho Brahe   60
8. The *New Astronomy*   67
9. First Steps in Celestial Mechanics   76
10. The Philosophy of Astrology   81
11. Thoughts on Light   87
12. The New Star of 1604   97
13. Comets and Sunspots   107
14. The Triumphs of the Telescope   114
15. From Prague to Linz   125
16. Measuring Time and Wine   131
17. The Witch Trial   139
18. The *Harmony of the Universe*   144
19. The *Epitome of Copernican Astronomy*   152

CONTENTS

20. From Linz to Ulm; the *Rudolphine Tables*   *page* 163

21. From Ulm to Sagan   168

22. Kepler's 'Dream'; Regensburg; the End of the Road   173

23. Conclusion   179

    Glossary   189

    Index   191

ILLUSTRATIONS

PLATES

John Kepler	*facing page* 48
Tycho Brahe	49
Galileo Galilei	64
Frontispiece of the *Rudolphine Tables*	65

FIGURES

1. The Eccentric Circle   *page* 35
2. Epicycle and Deferent   36
3. A Classic Planetary Theory   36
4. The Five Regular Solids   44
5. Kepler's Astronomical Application of the Regular Solids   46
6. Kepler's Hypothetical Circular Orbit for Mars   69
7. Kepler's Solution of the Problem of Mars   73
8. The Horoscope of Wallenstein   84
9. Kepler's Method of Determining the Refraction of Light by Glass   122
10. Finding the Volume of an Anchor-Ring   136
11. Kepler's Idea of the Sun's Action on a Planet   160

CHAPTER ONE

AN ANCIENT QUEST

W e have all become so familiar with the scientist's explanation of the course of natural events, and so conditioned by the pattern of life imposed upon us by a scientific technology, that we are apt to forget how recently, even on the scale of human history, our conventionally accepted world-picture was established. Yet if we could travel backward in time through but a few centuries we should find men, the best-informed of their age, confronting the Universe with presuppositions very different from those that prevail among us today. They would maintain that they occupied a privileged, central position in a closed, finite world designed to minister to their needs and to further their eternal destiny. And they would assert that that world was organized in a way that corresponded to the workings of their senses and minds so as to be completely perceptible and intelligible to human comprehension.

Within the last four hundred years these ideas have been disestablished by a new assessment of experience. The closed Universe of medieval Christendom has dissolved into the unbounded spaces of the modern cosmologist. Man has come to be regarded, at least at the natural level, as a recent and transient by-product of an order of nature heedless of his welfare and in which he plays an insignificant role, his faculties selectively adapted to ensure his biological survival rather than to afford him a synoptic vision of reality. And if, never-theless, he still strives to interpret experience, it is no longer in terms of properties and relations naïvely apprehended, but by reference to abstruse physical concepts—energy, entropy, action and the like—seemingly as mysterious as the events they are designed to rationalize.

This intellectual transformation was promoted by the rise of a new spirit of inquiry challenging long-established authority over wide areas of human concern. Traces of such a critical reaction had appeared in the late Middle Ages; and many factors conspired to bring it to fruition. But when the crucial phase of the movement was reached, contributions of decisive importance were made by the labours of a few men of genius, diverse in nationality, in mental endowment and in outlook, but each supplying some vital element to the new world-view that was coming into being. One of these men was the German astronomer John Kepler, whose life and labours form the subject of this book. His life-span, almost equally divided between the sixteenth and the seventeenth centuries, covered the middle course of what has come to be called the Scientific Revolution, and his writings reflect its onward march. In his voluminous treatises and letters, Kepler stands revealed to us as a man such as no other age could have produced. He still looks back to draw inspiration from the early stirrings of Greek natural philosophy; he clings to many preconceptions of the expiring Middle Ages; yet his working ideas anticipate the modern mechanistic approach to the physical world.

Kepler stands in the historic succession of those who, from the earliest ages of recorded history, have striven to discover consistency and meaning in the crude facts of experience. It is this ideal that has inspired the age-long attempts to visualize the architecture of the Universe and to reconstruct in imagination the process by which the whole scheme of things might have come into being. This introductory chapter will afford us an opportunity for glancing briefly at the roll of pioneers in this ancient quest and for noting the rise of some of the ideas that were to obstruct or inspire the workings of Kepler's mind. We shall take a closer look at the specific technical problems that confronted him when we reach the point where these become relevant.

The earliest cosmological affirmations that have come down to us from the ancient world, like those deriving from primitive peoples of our own day, are expressed in the language of myth. Cosmic origins and structures are explained on analogies drawn from more familiar domains of human experience. The Universe is pictured as a mere extension of the local geographical setting. It is conceived to have originated as an artefact, or as the offspring of some primeval mating, or as a community subjected to social order by some transcendent authority, or as a complete creation called into being out of nothing by the fiat of the Ancient of days.

The Babylonians imagined themselves to be living on the slopes of a huge hill planted upon the great deep and set within a sea-moat beyond which lay a circular mountain-wall supporting the solid firmament of the heavens. With its underworld abode of the dead and its 'waters above the firmament', this cosmology differs little from that pre-supposed in the Old Testament; it also suggests the world of Homer and Hesiod, ringed about with the stream of Ocean. The ancient Egyptians seem to have pictured themselves as living in a sort of elongated box extending towards the source of the Nile and bounded by the mountainous homelands of alien nations. The Earth floated above a watery underworld; it was surmounted by the over-arching heavens, which could be conceived as a solid vault upheld by four posts, or as a cow standing squarely, or as a goddess supporting herself on hands and feet. Each day the Sun-God sailed across the sky in a celestial boat, visiting the underworld by night; or the bright solar disc was rolled along by a scarab beetle.

The Greek natural philosophers of the sixth century before Christ and onwards swept all such creation myths away, apart from merely verbal vestiges. They concerned themselves with the physical processes, available to common observation or utilized in industry, that appeared to maintain the world in operation and that might have brought it into existence. Such an approach to experience lent itself to a materialistic view of life and a denial of purpose in the world. These tendencies found their extreme expression in the teachings of the Atomists, who conceived the Universe as a limitless void populated by an infinity of indestructible atoms, all alike in quality but differing in shape, position and arrangement. Flitting eternally through space, these atoms, by their fortuitous concourse, give rise to the Earth and its celestial neighbours and to an infinity of other such systems, which subsist only until the constituent atoms fall apart again. In such a system, order is statistical, not purposive.

The Atomist hypothesis was to be brought again into effective use by the pioneers of modern science; but for some two thousand years it remained eclipsed by a very different kind of philosophy that discovered a purposive order at the heart of reality, and that lent itself, when the time was ripe, to being harmonized with Christian theology. This philosophical reaction originated as an attempt to solve the problem of explaining how any knowledge worth the name could exist in a world which our senses present to us as subject to unceasing change. It might appear impossible to make clear-cut and permanently valid statements about such a confused medley of events and so to create a *science* of nature. The Athenian philosopher Plato (427–347 B.C.), following his teacher Socrates, sought a way out of this difficulty by conceiving as the proper objects of knowledge the eternal and self-existent Ideas, or *natures*, apprehended by the understanding and not by sense, and by participation in which an object of sense is characterized and made recognizable as the kind of thing it is and endowed with a fleeting existence at its appropriate level of reality. We are accustomed to think in this way whenever we study geometry, where our concern is with *perfect* straight lines, circles and so forth, and not with the more or less crude diagrams that serve us merely as aids to thought.

Plato may well have been inspired by the teachings of Pythagoras of Samos and his disciples who, in the sixth century before Christ, had begun to construct from such ideal elements the propositional geometry we know today. From Pythagoras and his school can be traced, as a recurring theme in later scientific thought, the conviction that the essential truth about the physical Universe is to be expressed, not in the imagery of myth, nor in analogy to crude material processes, but in the formal statement of the mathematical relations underlying natural phenomena. Tradition credits Pythagoras himself with the discovery that simple ratios connect the lengths of the segments of a vibrating lyre string that would give off musical notes forming a harmonious chord. Indeed, he seems to have taught that the distances of the several planets from the central Earth were as the lengths of such congruent segments, and even that the planets in their courses emitted a tuneful 'harmony of the spheres'. It was the Pythagoreans who first held up for the consideration and admiration of geometers the so-called 'regular solids', deemed by the youthful Kepler to embody specifications according to which the Creator fashioned the solar system. It was characteristic of the Pythagoreans that they represented numbers by sets of points spaced out and arranged to form simple geometrical figures. These could be conceived as built up to form solid bodies, or even to constitute space itself, so that, as the adherents of the Pythagorean School maintained, 'all things are number'.

The relevance of all this to our study of Kepler will become apparent when we see how his scientific endeavour reflected the revival that occurred at the Renaissance (particularly in southern Europe) of the Platonic philosophy, with all its Pythagorean overtones. In this revival Kepler eagerly participated, though he Christianized whatever he took from pagan thought. For him the Ideas became eternal 'archetypes' in the mind of God, serving Him as a pattern when He fashioned the material creation. However, in embracing this world-view, Kepler had to contend with the established philosophy of his day. For a thousand years and more the inspiration of Plato's teaching had been largely overshadowed by the authority of his sometime disciple Aristotle (384–322 B.C.), who denied the existence of a transcendental world of Ideas. For Aristotle the eternal natures were embodied in matter, from which they could be abstracted only in thought; and this was still the view of conservative philosophers in Kepler's day.

Plato and Aristotle each constructed a world-picture in accordance with his own characteristic outlook. Plato's was a geometer's world of perfect forms turned on the Creator's lathe. Yet it was also a living creature, artfully fashioned; and this dual conception was to be an essential element in Kepler's philosophy of nature. Aristotle's distinction as a naturalist has only lately been appreciated; and his was a biologist's universe, an organism in which the parts were subordinated to the perfect working of the whole. It was with Aristotle's world-view, transmitted through the ages with comparatively little modification, that the pioneers of modern astronomy had to contend; and some general account of it must be given here.

Aristotle pictured the Universe as a finite sphere, having nothing outside it, not even empty space, and built up within of concentric spheres like the skins of an onion. The stars were fixed to one of the outer spheres, which rotated once in a day. The seven 'planets', as the ancients understood the term, were conceived to be carried round the heavens by means of a manifold of revolving spheres: this method of representing the planetary motions had been thought out by another of Plato's disciples, Eudoxus of Cnidus. Everything within the Moon's sphere was composed of the four mutually convertible 'elements', earth, water, air and fire, forming, in that order, the solid ground, the ocean, the atmosphere and its supposed fiery envelope. Beyond the Moon's sphere everything was composed of the incorruptible aether. By their nature, elementary bodies tended to travel in straight lines towards (or away from) the centre of the Universe (which was also that of the Earth), while the celestial spheres eternally revolved about that centre.

Aristotle's crude representation of the planetary motions was soon superseded for purposes of practical astronomy by a purely geometrical technique, unrestricted by conformity to physical considerations and designed to facilitate the computation of tables for predicting the positions of the planets in the sky for years ahead. This technique reached its highest development at the hands of Ptolemy of Alexandria (second century A.D.), whose system of astronomy (firmly locating the Earth at the centre of the Universe) retained its authority during some fourteen centuries.

In Europe the ancient, essentially Greek civilization foundered about the fifth century A.D.; but the main philosophical traditions somehow survived to re-enter the stream of Western thought at various epochs. The cosmological ideas of Plato were the earliest to revive; towards the end of the ninth century they began to exert a predominant influence in Christendom. Meanwhile the twofold heritage of Aristotelian natural philosophy and Ptolemaic astronomy had passed to the Islamic civilization. By the twelfth century Graeco-Arabic science had begun to influence Western Christendom through the translation of many scientific classics from Arabic versions into Latin. The thirteenth century saw elaborate attempts to fuse Aristotelian natural philosophy with Christian theology in a great summation that was to command all but universal acceptance down to the seventeenth century. In the fifteenth century, and particularly in Italy and Germany, astronomical studies were powerfully stimulated by the recovery of Greek scientific texts in their original tongue and by the invention of printing. At the same time the needs of the pioneers of ocean navigation encouraged improvements in the design and construction of astronomical instruments, in the technique of celestial observation and in the calculation of tables.

Wider reading revealed that the bolder Greek thinkers had entertained very different ideas about the economy of the Universe from those eventually canonized by the authority of Aristotle and Ptolemy. Some had supposed the Universe infinite or had made the planetary train revolve, not about the Earth but about the Sun. A world-system involving such an inversion of the role of Sun and Earth, and relegating the Earth to a place among the planets, was constructed, in full numerical detail, in the mid-sixteenth century, about thirty years before Kepler was born. It was the life-work of the astronomer Nicholas Copernicus, whom Poles and Germans alike claim as a compatriot. The new system was opposed by conservative philosophers, both Catholic and Protestant, as being contrary to sound theology and physics and to the words of Scripture. Kepler was involved in this contest from his student days, and he never escaped from it.

In the wider spheres of politics and religious controversy the whole course of Kepler's life was shaped and too often distorted by the calamities and persecutions that marked that period of history. The Holy Roman Empire had long embraced in a formal unity, under the joint authority of Pope and Emperor, an assortment of peoples, united in a nominal Christianity but diverse in origin, temperament and circumstances. Nationalistic self-awareness and sectarian dissension were now forcing these peoples apart. The religious situation continued throughout Kepler's lifetime to be dominated by the cataclysm of the Reformation: the customary name reflects the more spiritual motives behind a complex movement. The late Middle Ages had seen many protests against the uses made by the Church of its wealth and power; and there had been occasional deviations from orthodoxy in search of a more Scriptural faith, as well as much anti-clerical satire. The New Learning, too, had played its part by revealing the Hebrew and Greek originals behind the priestly Latin of the Vulgate and by giving the layman the Bible in his native tongue. Religious discontent was brought to a head in Germany in 1517 when Martin Luther denounced the abuses connected with the sale of indulgences. Luther may originally have intended no general attack upon the authority of the Church; but the stress he laid upon the Pauline doctrine of justification by faith alone had the effect of bypassing the priestly office on the path to salvation.

The Protestant opposition to the authority of Rome did not crystallize into a single reformed Church. It divided broadly along national lines, following the lead of Luther in Germany, of Zwingli in Switzerland, and of Calvin in France.

Bitter theological conflicts arose between these rival confessions, particularly concerning the way in which the Sacrament was to be understood now that the Catholic doctrine of the Mass had been forsaken. These conflicts flared up within Germany, where the Calvinist teaching had secured a foothold. And though the Reformers had asserted the right of private judgement against ecclesiastical authority, they permitted their own followers no latitude in matters of belief. Moreover, the secular princes had inevitably become involved in the religious struggle, if only as claimants to the expropriated wealth of the Church. Kepler was tossed about by these contending parties and forced to take account of the differing persuasions of the princes he served. As a devout Protestant, he was repeatedly forced to flee from persecution at the hands of Catholic authorities. But when he betook himself to some region where the Lutheran faith was tolerated his troubles were not at an end. For he dissented from what had come to be the Lutheran doctrine of the Sacrament and suffered serious civil and spiritual disabilities in consequence. Like millions in our own day, Kepler led a restless, harassed existence which shortened his life and diminished his achievements.

CHAPTER TWO

SEED-TIME

John Kepler was born, a seven-months' child, on 27 December 1571 in south-west Germany. His birth-place was the Swabian town of Weil, or Weil-der-Stadt, barely to be found on a modern map, but enjoying in those days the privileges of a free Imperial city set in the Duchy of Württemberg. In its general appearance, the place can have changed but little with the passing centuries. The narrow streets and gabled houses still crowd round the steepled church crowning the low ridge beside the river Würm. Beyond the ruined walls, gardens and meadows roll away towards the Black Forest. Only today the broad market-place contains a memorial statue of Weil's most famous townsman.

The future astronomer was the firstborn child of Henry and Katherine Kepler; and because his birth fell on St. John's day he received the Apostle's name in baptism. On his father's side he came of an old Nuremberg family, ennobled in the fifteenth century for military services to the Emperor. But his more immediate ancestors had been settled in Swabia for some fifty years; they were now of bourgeois standing, and from their ranks Weil-der-Stadt had drawn several of its councillors and magistrates. His mother was the daughter of Melchior Guldenmann, the innkeeper and mayor of the neighbouring village of Eltingen.

The boy was born into an atmosphere of discord and insecurity from which he was never to escape. His parents were an ill-matched couple. The father was a man of evil temper who yearned for military adventure and kept volunteering for service in the Low Countries and elsewhere; it was while returning from some such campaign that he finally disappeared. His wife Katherine seems to have been a restless, quarrelsome woman, a believer in magic and herb lore, whom later it seemed quite natural to accuse of witchcraft. And this odd streak reappeared as part of the complex make-up of her famous son, who took after her also in his slender frame and dark hair and eyes.

There were six other children of the marriage, of whom three reached maturity: Henry, who went soldiering like his father; Margaret, who married a clergyman; and Christopher, who settled for a craftsman's life as a worker in pewter. For a time the young family was forsaken by both father and mother, and John was cared for by his grandparents, who showed him but little affection. He endured many childish ailments, barely surviving an attack of smallpox.

The domestic broils that troubled the astronomer's infancy were set in the wider context of the religious strife of the age. Living in a generally Catholic community, the Keplers belonged to a small Lutheran minority that was painfully struggling for freedom of belief and worship. But it remains uncertain into which faith the boy was baptized, the parish registers having been destroyed during the Thirty Years' War.

Following the Reformation, Latin schools had been founded up and down Württemberg, under ducal patronage, to take the place of the former monastic schools. They were designed to educate promising lads for the Church and the civil service. As a boy of seven, Kepler, already marked out by precocious talent, entered the Latin school at Leonberg, where the family was then living. Naturally, in these schools Latin studies took pride of place; and Kepler began to acquire that fluency in reading, writing and speaking the ancient language which used to distinguish the professional scholar and form an essential part of his technical equipment. The boys worked through the dull grammatical drill up to the point where they could tackle the classical texts of the old Roman authors; and meanwhile, as in the English public schools of the age, they were required to practise their Latin conversation on one another. The art of composition in German was rather neglected, so that the accomplished Latin of Kepler's major scientific treatises and formal letters contrasts with the crabbed German of his more popular works and with the curious mixture of Latin and German into which he often dropped.

Kepler's schooling should have been completed in three years, but it dragged on for five because the family kept moving from place to place. For a time the father tried his hand at running an inn at Ellmendingen and set his boy to hard labour on the land. It was at this period, however, that two events occurred that, as Kepler afterwards recalled, helped to awaken his interest in astronomy. His mother showed him the great comet of 1577, an apparition terrifying to the superstitious but highly instructive to the astronomers. And in 1580 his father took him out one night to see an eclipse of the Moon. So, as if by some pre-ordained compulsion of the kind he later loved to trace, and amid the squalor of his broken home, Kepler began in youth to turn his thoughts towards those celestial mysteries that were to be his lifelong concern. But not less marked or early manifested than the boy's astronomical predilections was his devoutly religious attitude to life and to the wonders of nature; so that when at length he left the Latin school, and his future career was under consideration, it seemed good to his parents and teachers that he should study to enter the Protestant ministry.

Kepler's goal was now the University of Tübingen, to be attained through successful studies at one or other of the preparatory seminaries that had been established in Swabia by the Protestant Dukes of Württemberg. These institutions were organized into two grades. The more elementary put a final polish upon the accomplishments acquired in the Latin schools, to which proficiency in Greek was now added; they led on to those of higher grade providing more specialized preparation for the University courses in arts and theology. The seminaries were often housed in former monasteries from which the monks had been ejected; such were those that Kepler attended. Under a director who still bore the title of Abbot, and subjected to something like the old monastic discipline, the seminarists were kept hard at work from morning till night. It was late in 1584 when Kepler, now close upon thirteen years of age, passed by competitive examination into the convent grammar school of Adelberg; thence he proceeded two years later into the senior seminary at Maulbronn.

In later years, looking back over his boyhood, Kepler wrote down what he could remember of its vicissitudes and tried to present his own self-portrait. He was not the sort of boy who is universally popular with his class-mates. Sometimes he would be lost in his own thoughts, hypnotized upon a world within or tormented by a morbidly sensitive conscience at the remembrance of some real or fancied sin. Yet he was responsive and vulnerable to the rough-and-tumble life around him; passionate both in friendship and in enmity; by turns aggressive, arrogant, servile. His distinction as a student aroused the jealousy of those less gifted or less industrious; his abhorrence of wrong-doing impelled him to report the lapses of the other scholars; his physical frailty made him an easy victim of schoolboy violence. He pondered much on the unsearchable mysteries of his Christian faith—on transubstantiation, predestination, the fate of the unevangelized heathen—and he already felt drawn to beliefs that were not those approved by the authorities with whom he had to deal. Much of Kepler's temperamental instability in adult life may be traced to the circumstances of his childhood—his broken home and unpresentable parents; his poverty and chronic ill-health, from which he had escaped only to enter the spiritual hothouse of the seminary.

CHAPTER THREE

TÜBINGEN AND GRAZ

I t was in the autumn of 1589 that Kepler entered the University of Tübingen, already famous as a centre of Protestant theological studies. Founded in 1477 by the first Duke of Württemberg, it had numbered Reuchlin the Humanist and Melanchthon the Reformer among its teachers; in the nineteenth century it was to become the seed-bed of the 'Tübingen School' of New Testament criticism. Already a bold, speculative, disputatious spirit pervaded the *Stift*—the 'Chapter'—as the theological seminary had come to be called, for it was housed in an old Augustinian monastery. As was the rule for divinity students, Kepler spent the first two years on a course in the Faculty of Arts, leading in 1591 to the Master's degree. This was followed by three more years devoted to the study of strictly theological subjects. The apprenticeship in Arts was quite to Kepler's taste, for, like many other brilliant boys who eventually settle for science (one thinks of Davy and Ampère, to name but two), he showed an early delight in flowery poetical composition, in the hyperbolic and the paradoxical.

For a student of those days, Kepler lived a very sober life. For one thing, he was educated on scholarships; his parents neither would nor could have contributed much to his school and university fees. For pocket money he depended upon various forms of bounty and so missed much youthful fun. In any case, the seminarists were naturally subjected to a stricter discipline than the other students: they would some day be clergymen and must not be allowed to participate in undergraduate debaucheries. However, one of his few relaxations was amateur dramatics; he took part in student plays, generally on biblical themes, in which, being slightly built, he was chosen to play female parts. It was only to be expected, too, that Kepler, preoccupied as he already was with the celestial domain, should be caught up in the prevailing practice of astrological prediction. Already in his student days he became known for his skill in casting horoscopes, though he was soon to outgrow the cruder forms of this superstition.

Besides the classical languages, ethics and so forth, the arts course at Tübingen significantly included astronomy. And of all Kepler's teachers, it was Michael Mästlin, the professor of mathematics and astronomy, whose influence upon him was to prove the most momentous. Born at Göppingen near Stuttgart in or about 1550 and destined for the Protestant ministry, Mästlin, too, had studied theology at Tübingen, where he attended the mathematical lectures of Philip Apian the cartographer and developed scientific interests to which he devoted his leisure after his appointment as Deacon of Backnang in Swabia. Mästlin had already begun to win fame through his astronomical writings when, in 1580, he was called to be professor at Heidelberg. Three years later he had come to occupy the Tübingen Chair rendered vacant by the dismissal of his former teacher Apian for refusing to subscribe to some formulary of the Lutheran faith. Mästlin retained this post until his death in 1631, the year following the decease of his most famous pupil. He was one of the observers who had established that the 'new star' of 1572 exhibited no measurable diurnal parallax and must therefore be located in the celestial spaces beyond the Moon. He drew a comparable conclusion about the great comet of 1577. Mästlin was aware of the advantages that the Copernican theory had to offer astronomers, but he was afraid to embrace it too openly; only in the later editions of his *Epitome of Astronomy* did he make unobtrusive mention of its startling reversal of long-accepted ideas in cosmology.

However, his gifted disciple eagerly picked up the hints in the master's lectures. Writing a few years later, Kepler relates how 'when I was at Tübingen six years ago, studying under the renowned master Michael Mästlin, I was impressed by the manifold inconvenience of the customary opinion concerning the Universe; and I took such delight in Copernicus, of whom Mästlin, in his lectures, used to make frequent mention, that I not only used often to defend the doctrines of Copernicus in the candidates' disputations on physics, but I also composed a careful argument concerning that *first motion* which arises from the rotation of the Earth'. Kepler continued in correspondence with Mästlin in after years, consulting him on the various technical problems that he encountered in the course of his lifelong endeavour for astronomy.

Kepler was not destined after all to complete his Tübingen studies or to enter the Church. Early in 1594 the University authorities were asked to recommend a suitable teacher of mathematics for the Protestant seminary at Graz in Styria to fill the post left vacant by the death of Georg Stadius. The Senate nominated Kepler. The choice was a tribute to his distinction as a student; but it is possible that Kepler's teachers may have entertained some doubts as to whether he would be wise to enter the Lutheran ministry. In those far-off days a clergyman was expected to believe and to preach the doctrines that he professed at his ordination; and in the opinion of strict Lutherans Kepler may not have appeared completely 'sound'. So they may have thought they were doing him a kindness in switching him into a teaching post. For his part, Kepler felt bound to accept the appointment, though determined not to forgo permanently his sacred vocation. He left Tübingen in March 1594.

In migrating to Graz, Kepler moved into an atmosphere of religious conflict such as he had never encountered in his Lutheran homeland of Württemberg. While the nobles and the bourgeoisie favoured the reformed religion, the Archduke Charles, under whose rule had fallen the south-western provinces of a divided Austria, had summoned the Jesuits to Graz to begin a Catholic re-conquest of Styria, to be continued by his widow and his son, the Archduke Ferdinand.

The Graz seminary had been established in 1574; intended primarily for educating the sons of the nobility, it also received those of the townsfolk and it had become the local stronghold of Protestantism. Kepler was to be responsible for the instruction in mathematics and astronomy; but he was an exacting teacher and these subjects were not very popular with his youthful charges and their philistine progenitors. He soon lacked pupils, and his teaching activities had to be broadened out to cover other branches of the curriculum. His appointment also carried with it the offices of District Mathematician (a sort of borough surveyor) and maker of calendars, so that he did not want for occupation. Moreover, his social contacts were widened through these official duties and through the universal interest in astrological prediction which he was in a position to gratify in some measure. Kepler published calendars for each of the six years 1595 to 1600 of his residence in Graz. These calendars were no mere registers of months and days and festivals; they gave the dates of predictable celestial events such as phases of the Moon, eclipses, planetary phenomena, but also, more questionably, prospects for the weather and harvest, and advice on when to gather medicinal herbs. They announced the fate of kingdoms and the fortunes of war, all as foreshown astrologically by the aspects of the planets. When Kepler arrived in Graz he found that the fame of his Tübingen vaticinations had preceded him; and his reputation as an astrologer was further enhanced when, in his first calendar, he foretold a spell of severe weather and a Turkish invasion, both of which came to pass. He was, indeed, highly sceptical of the elaborate rules of contemporary astrology. He condemned much that he found extravagant and superstitious in the popular forms of the false science; and he made some show of preparing his prognostications under protest. But he was not among the few of his time who completely rejected astrology on scientific or theological grounds. We shall have more to say later about Kepler's mature philosophy of astrology and about the controversies in which he became involved with opponents more credulous or more sceptical than himself.

However, Kepler's meditations were now soaring high above this popular misreading of what the heavens declare; and his thoughts continued to dwell upon the Copernican planetary scheme not only for its intrinsic beauty but also in the conviction that it could afford hitherto undreamt-of insights into the order of nature. For one thing, Copernicus had shown how to determine by observation the relative distances of the planets from the centre of the solar system, which no astronomer before him had been able to do. So there was now a hope of establishing some mathematically significant relation between these distances such as the Greek astronomers had imagined to subsist. We must now interrupt our narrative of Kepler's career to turn the pages of his first great book in which this idea was worked out. First, however, it will be useful to take a preparatory glance at the state of planetary astronomy in Kepler's day.

CHAPTER FOUR

PLANETARY PROBLEMS

Kepler was born in an age when the sciences, after a thousand years of largely misdirected effort, were at last being set again upon the onward road. To this process of reorientation he was to make major and manifold contributions that will claim our attention time and again in the following pages. But his supreme achievements lay in the field of planetary astronomy where, after following several false trails, he at length arrived at what has proved to be a precise and valid description of *how* an undisturbed planet would revolve round the Sun. It fell to Kepler also to take the first steps towards explaining on mechanical principles *why* a planet revolves in an orbit at all. With Kepler about to make his first attack upon the problem of the planets, it may be useful at this point to trace how planetary theory developed to the stage at which it first awakened his youthful curiosity.

Too early for historical record the distinction was drawn between the stars, ranged in enduring constellations over the night sky, and the planets, wandering across the backcloth of stars. The early watchers of the heavens learned to identify the brighter stars and the more striking star groups, or constellations; and they knew five of the major planets, the ones we call Mercury, Venus, Mars, Jupiter and Saturn. These they classed with the Sun and the Moon (which also travel round the sky) to make up the seven 'planets' in the wider sense in which the word was understood in the Middle Ages. They took account of the motions of these planets, partly as an aid to reckoning times and seasons, partly as a means of divination. But even where utility was not involved they felt the scientific compulsion to reduce to a rule this most impressive of all the manifestations of the orderliness of nature. And in this they were the spiritual ancestors of Kepler and of all astronomers down to our own day.

To look now at the planetary motions in some detail: the most obvious, affecting all the heavenly bodies including the stars, is that which daily carries them all (and most conspicuously the Sun) across the sky from east to west. It is as if they were all distributed over the interior of a 'celestial sphere' having the observer at its centre and turning once a day about one of its diameters. However, while all sharing in this daily westward motion, the seven 'planets' were also found to show an eastward drift through the constellations. They travel slowly round the heavens, each in its characteristic period of revolution—the Moon in one lunar month, the Sun (with Mercury and Venus) in one year, and (in round numbers) Mars in two years, Jupiter in twelve years and Saturn in thirty years. This motion is not perfectly uniform: a planet's daily travel fluctuates slightly about its mean value within the planet's period of revolution, this non-uniformity being called its *first inequality*. Mercury and Venus show the further peculiarity that the angular distance of each from the Sun never exceeds a certain moderate limit. And, to complicate matters further, the five planets (in the modern restricted sense) do not, like the Sun and Moon, travel continuously eastward among the constellations. The motion of each is arrested and reversed at fairly regular intervals, and it travels westwards for some weeks through an 'arc of retrogression' before resuming its eastward course. This is the planet's *second in-*

equality. The ancient astronomers learned to disentangle these two inequalities by observing the planet when it was 'in opposition' to the Sun, that is, when the Sun, the Earth and the planet lay roughly in a straight line, for then the second inequality vanishes.

The two historic civilizations (at least of classical times) that did most to reduce the planetary motions to a system were the Babylonian and the Greek. The Babylonians computed planetary ephemerides, or time-tables, of considerable refinement; but it was the Greeks who originated the great tradition of geometrical and physical astronomy that descended through many schools to Kepler and which he was to transform decisively. It was, by tradition, Pythagoras of Samos and his disciples who, in the sixth century before Christ, first applied an elegant mathematical technique to the problems of astronomy.

Whereas the Earth had at first been pictured as a flat disk surrounded by the ocean, the Pythagoreans, whether from physical or from aesthetic considerations, ascribed to it the perfect symmetry of a sphere; and this view has never since been seriously contested. The spherical Earth was conventionally located at the centre of a finite, spherical Universe; and this conception of an Earth-centred cosmos was not seriously questioned until the middle of the sixteenth century. Again, the Sun, varying the height of its diurnal arc with the changing seasons, appears in the course of a year to describe round the heavens a closely woven spiral; but the Pythagoreans realized that this complicated curve could be resolved into two uniform circular motions. The first of these carried the Sun round the heavens from west to east in one year, and the second, common to all the heavenly bodies and inclined to the plane of the first, carried the Sun round from east to west once every day. This artifice also served to represent, somewhat crudely, the motions of the Moon and of the five planets, so that it is not surprising that the ancient Greek natural philosophers laid it down that the apparently complicated movements of the heavenly bodies consisted of combinations of uniform circular motions into which it was the task of the astronomer to resolve them. This doctrine persisted until Kepler's day; and he was the first formally to set it aside.

Plato's planetary system was just such a Pythagorean one, taking no account of the retrogressions of the planets, but setting these bodies to revolve about the central Earth at distances arbitrarily fixed to conform to a trivial arithmetical rule. However, Plato did set the astronomers of his day the task of representing the actual motions of the planets more realistically by assigning to them further combinations of circular motions in divers planes having the Earth at their common centre. And this problem was solved, as we have seen, to a certain degree of approximation, by one of Plato's own disciples, Eudoxus of Cnidus. What may originally have been conceived as an ideal geometrical construction became, in Aristotle's world-system, a material mechanism designed to keep the planets moving in their appointed courses. The so-called 'spheres of Eudoxus' were revised and re-fashioned from time to time up to within half a century of Kepler's birth. However, the hypothesis of spheres took no account of the first inequality, or of variations in a planet's distance from us betokened by recurrent changes in its brightness. And so Greek astronomers of the later, Alexandrian period broke free from some of the physical restrictions imposed by Aristotle in their efforts to reproduce and so in some sense to account for the observed behaviour of a typical planet.

The Greek astronomers, in fact, established the practice of representing the planet by a point tracing out some specified curve in space relatively to a fixed central point corresponding to the Earth, where the observer was supposed to be situated. The problem was treated as a purely kinematic one, taking into consideration distances and angles, times and speeds, but making no reference to forces supposed to impel or restrain the planet. And that was the way in which the problem was still being tackled when Kepler took it in hand some two thousand years later.

Let us look now at the typical devices employed in classical planetary theories prior to Kepler's reformation of astronomy, taking no account for the moment of the diurnal motion common to all the celestial bodies.

The construction that best suited the Sun's apparent motion was the *eccentric circle*, in which the centre C of the Suns' circular orbit was displaced some distance from the Earth E (Fig. 1). Viewed from the Earth, the Sun S appeared to be

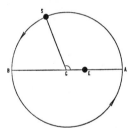

1. The Eccentric Circle

moving most rapidly through the constellations when at A and slowest when at B. On the other hand, to account for the phenomenon of retrogression in the planets, the Greek astronomers placed the planet P on a small circle (the *epicycle*) whose centre O described a larger circle (the *deferent*) about the central Earth E (Fig. 2). By a suitable adjustment of the radii of the circles and the speeds of the moving points, the planet could be made to exhibit a retrograde motion when it was in the neighbourhood of A, the point of its nearest approach to the Earth. These two devices could be combined to

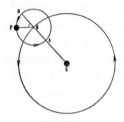

2. Epicycle and Deferent

give the planet an eccentric deferent. Or a planet's motion could be reproduced even more realistically by making the angular velocity of O uniform, not about the Earth E or the centre C, but about an arbitrarily chosen *equant point* H, found by experience to be most advantageously situated where CH = CE (Fig. 3). Then O, P moved so that the angles

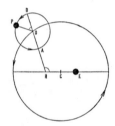

3. A Classic Planetary Theory

CHO, POB increased uniformly with the lapse of time. That, in fact, came to be the usual set-up for a planet, providing for both the first and the second inequalities.

This system of geometrical astronomy was summed up in the second century A.D. by Ptolemy of Alexandria in a book that came to be known as the *Almagest*. The Arabs and their subject peoples preserved and worked over this classical tradition without appreciably enriching it; though they sometimes conceived the planetary systems in mechanical terms, with solid spheres to carry the planets round their epicycles and deferents.

PLANETARY PROBLEMS

In the middle of the sixteenth century, Nicholas Copernicus asserted that the Sun stood fixed at or near the centre of the Universe, that the five planets revolved round the Sun in roughly concentric circles, and that the Earth revolved with them in a sixth planetary orbit, situated between those of Venus and Mars. This hypothesis, published in 1543, immediately accounted for the Sun's apparent annual circuit through the heavens and all seasonal phenomena affecting the Earth. At the same time Copernicus postulated a daily eastward rotation of the Earth on its polar axis, thus explaining, as a mere appearance, the daily rising and setting of the heavenly bodies. However, the principal scientific advantage offered by the Copernican hypothesis was that it supplied an almost commonsense explanation of the periodic retrogressions of the planets and their concomitant variations in brightness that had puzzled astronomers for so many centuries. These could now be regarded as purely optical phenomena, the result of projecting on to the planet a motion that really belonged to the observer as the Earth carried him annually round the Sun. This meant the disappearance of the large epicycles that Ptolemy and his successors had been obliged to introduce into their geometrical schemes for the purpose of representing this peculiar feature of planetary behaviour. It was this gain in mathematical elegance that led the youthful Kepler wholeheartedly to embrace the new *heliocentric*, or 'Sun-centred', cosmology, when as yet only a minority of astronomers had done so.

Opposition to the Copernican theory came chiefly from the entrenched scholastic philosophy which embraced Christian theology, Aristotelian physics and Ptolemaic astronomy, the whole tinged with astrological preoccupations. Assertion of the Earth's motion was accounted by the Protestants as conflicting with the words of Scripture, and by the Catholics as opposed to the great scholastic synthesis of the thirteenth century, which had become the official philosophy of the Church. Ptolemy's planetary theory did not, indeed, strictly conform to Aristotle's physics; but all down the ages, practical astronomers, Alexandrian, Muslim and Christian alike, had surmounted this difficulty by treating the theory as a mere artifice to be utilized in the calculation of planetary tables without prejudice to the physical truth of the matter. Now a new option had appeared in the theory of Copernicus; tables based upon it were found to be rather more accurate than those previously in use, which helped to commend the theory to practical astronomers. But this improvement was the result of employing rather more accurate data; it had little to do with the underlying doctrine. Hence practitioners usually thought it best to treat this new theory, too, as a calculating device. For neither then nor for two centuries after, was there available a scrap of direct physical evidence to support the hypothesis of the Earth's motion. Experimental tests devised to settle the question one way or the other appeared, indeed, to decide against Copernicus; though, as became clear when sounder mechanical doctrines prevailed, such tests were bound to give the same negative result, within the limits of precision attainable, whether the Earth moved or not. On the other hand, celestial phenomena that might have afforded physical proof, at least of the Earth's annual revolution round the Sun, long remained imperceptible to even the most refined observation.

For example, the revolution of the Earth in an orbit ought to give rise to a corresponding periodic displacement in the apparent positions of the stars. For when an observer changes his point of observation all neighbouring objects show an opposite shift, or *parallax*, the more pronounced the nearer they are to the observer. Kepler, like all the other early Copernicans, was disappointed that no one had ever detected the eagerly sought phenomenon in the stars, reflecting the Earth's yearly revolution round the Sun. He was obliged to fall back on the stock excuse (which happened to be the true explanation) that the stars were too far away for this phenomenon to be discernible with the available instruments.

It therefore came as a relief to conservative astronomers when it was shown that the Copernican scheme could be inverted into a kinematically equivalent one in which the Earth was the fixed centre. The planets still revolved round the Sun, but the Sun (and the Moon) revolved round the Earth, and the whole Universe also revolved daily round the Earth. Such a 'geo-heliocentric' theory was announced in 1588 by the Danish astronomer Tycho Brahe, not as a calculating device but as a physical fact; and this compromise constituted an effective alternative to the Copernican theory during the latter part of Kepler's career, though he never adopted it. It retained its popularity through much of the seventeenth century, largely on account of the ban placed by the Church on theories involving the motion of the Earth.

To return, in conclusion, to the Copernican planetary scheme: the planets revolve at different distances from the Sun, represented by the radii of their respective circular orbits. Copernicus had shown how, by suitable observations, these distances could be determined, not in conventional units such as miles but in terms of the radius of the Earth's orbit. Several of the Greek philosophers, and notably Plato, had conceived the distances of the successive planets from the common centre of revolution (which they took to be the Earth) as forming a recognizable arithmetical sequence or as proportional to the lengths of lyre strings vibrating in some celestial harmony. In Alexandrian times this sort of thing gave place to the view, which we generally adopt today, that the dimensions of the planetary system are arbitrary specifications, to be determined where possible by combined observation and hypothesis. The Greek astronomers did, in fact, estimate the distances from us of the Moon (fairly accurately) and of the Sun (very inaccurately). However, during the Middle Ages another fanciful notion gained wide acceptance. Once it had been recognized that a planet regularly varies its distance from the Earth, it seemed natural to assign to each planet a 'sphere', or layer of space within which it was always to be found. This was the region confined between two spherical surfaces centred upon the Earth and whose radii were respectively equal to the greatest and to the least distance of the planet from the Earth. Certain medieval astronomers came to believe that these spheres were *contiguous*, the greatest distance of any one planet being equal to the least distance of the one next outside it. This arrangement was supposed to ensure that no space should be wasted, since nature does nothing in vain. When, in due course, Copernicus referred the planetary motions to the Sun (or, more strictly, to a point located near the Sun), he thereby greatly reduced the variations that had to be assumed in the distance of a planet from its centre of revolution and that constituted the thickness of its 'sphere'. He thus exploded this old idea that the 'spheres' of neighbouring planets were contiguous. For he showed that the greatest distance of one planet was not equal to the least distance of the next, so that once again astronomers were confronted with what seemed to be arbitrary numbers specifying the dimensions of the solar system. It was at this point that Kepler took up the problem.

CHAPTER FIVE

THE *COSMOGRAPHIC MYSTERY*

In hours spared from his theological studies at Tübingen,
Kepler had reflected upon the advantages enjoyed by the
Copernican over the Ptolemaic planetary theory. And in
his leisure time at Graz he had come to meditate upon the
three awesome problems of why there were six planets and
neither more nor less, why the planetary orbits were the size
they were, and why the planets described them in the periodic
times they did. He could not regard these specifications as
determined by chance; they must have been prescribed by the
Creator, the 'ever-geometrizing' God of Plato, to embody
some divine harmony to which the mind of the human
mathematician, too, is attuned. The Copernican theory
seemed to offer a deeper insight into the symmetries of the
planetary domain; and Kepler wove these two themes together to form the subject of his first notable book, the
Cosmographic Mystery (so to render its long Latin title), which
Mästlin saw through the press at Tübingen late in 1596. The
volume contains little of permanent scientific value, and yet
it is of great interest as embodying most of the fundamental
ideas that its author later developed in his major works.

It had been Kepler's original intention to begin his book
with a frank avowal of his belief in the Copernican theory,
and to maintain that it was not inconsistent with Scripture to
assign the central place to the Sun. But he yielded to the

counsel of the Tübingen authorities, with whose approval the work appeared, and agreed to treat the theory merely as a mathematical hypothesis leading to interesting results. By adopting this course he ensured that the book should be judged on its scientific merits only and that believers should not be scandalized. 'The whole of astronomy', he wrote, 'is not worth so much that one of Christ's little ones should be injured.'

What really convinced Kepler of the truth of the Copernican theory was not only its success in predicting celestial events, but even more the way in which it bound together in mathematical necessity what had previously appeared as the merely arbitrary phenomena of planetary motion. Copernicus alone had been able to account for the frequency of occurrence, the extent in angle and the duration in time of the retrogression that a superior planet exhibits from time to time in its normally eastward course through the constellations, and to explain why this always occurs when the planet is near opposition to the Sun. The large epicycle that Ptolemy had introduced into the economy of each of the superior planets was simply the reflex of the Earth's annual motion. Indeed, these epicycles appeared of just the same size as the Earth's orbit would have looked if it could have been surveyed from these planets in turn.

Kepler saw the Universe as made up of things at rest and things moving. The Sun, the fixed stars and the intervening space were at rest; and he held that a harmony subsisted between these three and the three Persons of the Trinity. It was a harmony and not merely an analogy, for the Trinity was an archetype of the Universe. He next sought for an answering harmony to embrace the moving parts of the Universe—the planets, in fact. It was natural for him to begin by looking for simple arithmetical relations connecting the radii of the planetary orbits, but nothing useful emerged even when he introduced two hypothetical planets, the one in the wide gap between Jupiter and Mars and the other between Venus and Mercury. He was no more successful with a supposed trigonometrical relation between a planet's distance from the Sun and the 'motive power' supposedly needed to carry it round the Sun in the time observed. Then one day in 1595 he was explaining to his students how the planet Jupiter, which performs a circuit of the heavens in about twelve years, periodically overtakes the planet Saturn, which requires about thirty years to get round, and how the place of such a conjunction of the planets works round the sky, jumping about 240° at a time. Drawing a circle to represent the zodiac, he joined the places of forty successive conjunctions by straight lines, and he found that these enveloped a smaller circle which seemed to stand to the larger as the orbit of Jupiter to that of Saturn. But this construction could not bear extension to the remaining planets, nor could it explain why there should be only six of these. In any case, plane figures seemed incongruous with the solid planetary spheres. However, the attempt put Kepler on to what he imagined was the right track. For six planets have *five* interspaces separating them one from another; and this suggested the *five* regular solids of the Greek geometers. The supposed relation of these solids to the planetary scheme forms the principal theme of Kepler's book.

The most familiar of the regular solids is the cube; and it may serve to illustrate the properties that characterize all five members of the class, shown in Figure 4. The six faces of the cube are all equal squares; its twenty-four plane angles are all equal, and so are its twelve edges and its eight corners (or solid angles). The other regular solids are the tetrahedron (bounded by four equilateral triangles), the octahedron (bounded by eight equilateral triangles), the dodecahedron

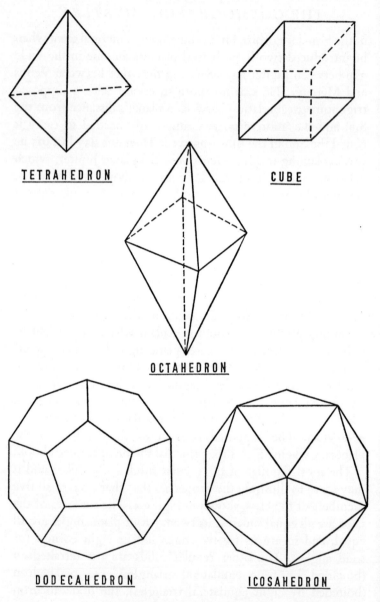

TETRAHEDRON

CUBE

OCTAHEDRON

DODECAHEDRON

ICOSAHEDRON

4. The Five Regular Solids

(bounded by twelve regular pentagons) and the icosahedron (bounded by twenty equilateral triangles). These five solids were discovered by the Greek geometers; Plato associated them with the fine structure of the four elements and the form of the Universe, whence they are often called the 'Platonic' figures (or bodies). Euclid had proved that there can be but five polyhedra possessing complete regularity of this kind. He had shown how to construct them geometrically, how to construct, too, their inscribed spheres (touching all the faces) and their circumscribed spheres (passing through all the vertices), and how to calculate for each of them the ratio of the 'in-radius' to the 'circum-radius'. There are *five* such ratios, one for each solid. Taking now the six planets in order, the greatest distance of one planet from the Sun stands to the least distance of the next outer planet in a fixed ratio; and here again there are *five* such ratios.

Kepler now surmised that the two sets of ratios, the planetary and the geometrical, might be identical. This would amount to saying that a regular solid could be interposed between two adjacent planets so that the inner planet, when at its greatest distance from the Sun, lay on the inscribed sphere of the solid, while the outer planet, when at its least distance, lay on the circumscribed sphere. And at first sight it seemed that, if the greatest distance of Mercury from the Sun were taken as the radius of the inscribed sphere of an octahedron, then the radius of the sphere circumscribed to it would just represent the least distance of Venus. Thus an octahedron could just be interposed between the orbits of Mercury and Venus. Similarly, the four other regular solids, the icosahedron, the dodecahedron, the tetrahedron and the cube, could, in that order, be interposed between the remaining five planets, Venus, Earth, Mars, Jupiter and Saturn (Fig. 5). This hypothesis had nothing to say about a planet's least

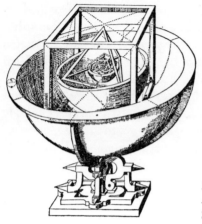

5. Kepler's Astronomical
Application of the Regular
Solids

and greatest distances from the Sun, which depended upon
the eccentricity of its orbit and which defined the thickness of
its 'sphere', the region of space within which the planet was
always to be found. And whether or not the Moon's orbit
should be included in the thickness of the Earth's 'sphere' was
a question that Kepler resolved to decide in the way that best
agreed with his planetary hypothesis.

Kepler naturally arranged the regular solids in the order
that best fitted the dimensions of the planetary spheres. But he
was not the man to regard this order as arbitrary; and his
attempts to account for it by an appeal to geometrical considerations anticipated in some measure the modern Principle
of Duality as it is exemplified in the properties of the regular
solids. Thus, the cube, tetrahedron and dodecahedron, which
lay outside the Earth's orbit, seemed to form a class distin-
guishable from the octahedron and icosahedron, which lay
within. The cube with its six faces and eight vertices, corresponded to the octahedron with its six vertices and eight faces;
the dodecahedron with its twelve faces and twenty vertices

corresponded to the icosahedron with its twelve vertices and twenty faces. (He might have added that the tetrahedron with its four faces and four vertices was self-corresponding.) Kepler also (if only as an astrological fantasy) linked the geometrical properties of the solids with the supposed good and evil qualities of their associated planets. But he later denied that planets could be evil in themselves, though he thought their influence might stimulate men to wickedness just as music might prompt them to dance.

When Kepler checked his hypothesis numerically against the actual specifications of the planetary system, as derived from observation, he found what he judged to be a significant measure of agreement. In any case, discrepancies were not conclusive evidence against the hypothesis, for no great reliance could be placed upon the figures supplied by Copernicus, who did not claim to be an outstanding observer. Copernicus had measured the planetary distances not from the Sun but from the centre of the Earth's orbit, which lay at some distance from the Sun; in consequence, the Earth's orbit exhibited no eccentricity and the Earth's 'sphere' (if the Moon were left out of account) possessed no thickness. Kepler thought a better agreement might be obtained by reckoning distances from the Sun itself. Mästlin carried out the necessary calculations, and though little seemed to be gained, this change of origin was of momentous importance for the subsequent development of Kepler's ideas.

If (as Mästlin pointed out to the Tübingen authorities) Kepler's hypothesis about the regular solids fitted the measured dimensions of the planetary spheres sufficiently closely, then it might be assumed that any discrepancies were entirely due to errors of observation and that in reality the fit was an exact one. In that event the relative distances of the planets could be obtained to any desired degree of precision by calculation alone, and no further measurements would be needed. Just as we might say that, once the analytical properties of the circle had been established, there was no longer any sense in determining the ratio of the circumference to the diameter by measurement. Indeed, in our own day, it has been claimed by physicists somewhat in the Kepler tradition that certain pure numbers representing combinations of fundamental physical quantities can be arrived at from very general considerations, yielding more accurate results than could possibly be obtained by experiment.

In a later chapter of his book Kepler seeks to explain why the periods of revolution of the planets show a progressive increase as we pass outward from Mercury to Saturn. His attempts to establish a relation between a planet's period and its distance from the Sun, though for the moment fruitless, were highly significant in view of the success that rewarded his later attack upon this problem. It was natural that an outer planet should require more time to complete a revolution than an inner one since it had to traverse a larger circuit. But it seemed that this was not the whole story. The speeds of the planets steadily diminish with increasing distance from the Sun, thereby lengthening the periods still further. Consideration of the speeds of the planets inevitably raised the problem of how the planets were maintained in motion. According to the mechanical ideas of Kepler's time (ideas that could be traced back to Aristotle) a continuous application of force was required to keep a body moving; if the force ceased the body came to rest. The traditional view had been that the planets were carried round by rotating spheres to which they were attached, the motion of the spheres being spontaneous (somewhat like the motion of an animal, which supplies its own motive force) or else maintained by some angelic agent. Kepler preferred to regard the planets as moving unfettered

John Kepler

Tycho Brahe

and unimpeded through the celestial spaces, impelled and directed by a certain 'divine force' and regulating their courses in obedience to geometrical principles. He supposed at first that each planet might possess in itself a 'motive soul' (*anima motrix*), or principle of motion, acting more feebly the further the planet was from the Sun, though in the notes that he appended to the second edition of his book he significantly substituted the word 'force' (*vis*) for 'soul', thus transforming a vague animistic fantasy into a manageable problem of mechanics.

Alternatively, there might be 'but a single motive soul in the centre of all the orbits, namely, in the Sun, which urges forward any body the more vehemently the nearer it is; upon the more remote bodies the force is in some degree weakened owing to the distance and the resulting attenuation of the virtue'. As for the way the Sun acts upon a planet, Kepler believed that there emanated from the luminary an 'immaterial species' (*species immateriata*). The term had a medieval connotation, and it had come to be applied to light, which enables the luminous source to be perceived at a distance through the (supposedly) instantaneous transmission of something which is not material. Kepler surmised that the Sun's driving force fell off with increasing distance according to the same law as that to which light was subject. And at this period he still believed that the intensity of light varied inversely as the simple distance from the luminous source and not (as he later correctly affirmed) inversely as the *square* of the distance from the source. Even so, probably for want of a clear mathematical notation, Kepler became involved in confusion when he tried to formulate the relation between the period of a planet and its distance from the Sun. And to secure a better agreement between his figures and the measured quantities themselves, he took into account the different sizes or weights of the several planets (somewhat fancifully estimated) which he supposed might have a bearing upon the resistances they would offer and thus might influence their speeds.

As a planet revolves in its eccentric orbit its distance from the Sun varies appreciably; on Kepler's suppositions this must produce corresponding fluctuations in the force acting upon the planet and hence in its speed. The planet must move most rapidly when nearest to the Sun; and this was in general agreement with Ptolemy's hypothesis of a symmetrically situated equant point, to which Kepler was inclined to return.

Kepler thought the world must have begun with the planets all drawn up in a line stretching out from the Sun towards the origin of the zodiac. In the closing pages of his 'Mystery' he reckoned that the heavens must have exhibited some such configuration about 5572 years before the year in which he was writing (1595), a remote epoch which might well have marked the Creation, when the newly formed planets stood ready to be launched upon their age-long courses. But he reckoned that the periods of revolution of the several planets could not be commensurable one with another so as to possess a least common multiple. Hence there could be no 'Platonic year' after which the Sun and his planetary train would all be lined up again, this time, perhaps, to announce the end of the world.

The *Cosmographic Mystery* enjoyed a mixed reception, the more philosophic readers commending its author for having assumed the mantle of Plato and the more empirically minded maintaining that such specifications as the distances of the planets could be determined only by measuring what there was to measure.

CHAPTER SIX

FROM GRAZ TO PRAGUE

W e must take up again the thread of Kepler's life-
story. Early in 1596 he returned to Württemberg
on two months' leave of absence. He took the
opportunity of calling on his two grandfathers, whose lives
were drawing to a close; he also consulted his old teacher
Michael Mästlin about the lay-out and publication of his
Cosmographic Mystery. He paid his respects to the Duke in
Stuttgart; he owed his start in life to a ducal scholarship and
now wished to show his gratitude to his old patron by presenting him with an elegant model of the new planetary
scheme of spheres and solids to add to his collection of curiosities. Plans for constructing the model came to nothing
because of technical difficulties; but the careful working-draw-
ing that Kepler prepared served as an illustration for his forthcoming book and afforded some visual aid to grasping his
planetary system. Kepler's attendance upon the Duke served
as his excuse for having long outstayed his leave when he
returned to Graz in August 1596. Kepler was inexperienced in
authorship and in the preparation of manuscripts for the
printer. So he was all the more indebted to Mästlin for making
his book even as lucid and intelligible to the lay reader as it
is, and still more for all the trouble the old mathematician
took in seeing it through the press at Tübingen.

As has been the custom of authors in all ages, Kepler gave

away many complimentary copies of his new book to friends and patrons and contemporary scholars, including fifty to Mästlin. One copy was sent to the Italian scientist Galileo Galilei and was the means of introducing the two men to each other. Their lives and studies were to touch at many points in after years, and they were to reach the highest level of attainment in much the same fields of study during the crucial phase of the Scientific Revolution. But so diverse were they in temperament and in scientific philosophy that the fruitful co-operation sought by Kepler, and from which so much of benefit might have resulted to their common studies, was never achieved.

Born at Pisa in 1564 and educated by the Jesuits, Galileo was now Professor of Mathematics at Padua, already meditating and experimenting on the motions of bodies under gravity and linking his results with the problem of the Earth's motion. Upon receiving, in August 1597, Kepler's gift of his book, Galileo replied in a few hours, declaring that he had embraced the opinion of Copernicus 'many years since' (at the time of writing he was thirty-three years of age). He has not yet had time to read the book (he writes) but he is keenly looking forward to doing so. 'This I will do the more gladly because I came round to the opinion of Copernicus many years ago, and, from that point of view, I arrived at the causes of many natural effects which are doubtless inexplicable according to the common hypothesis. I have written down many reasons in favour of it, and refutations of arguments for the contrary view; but I have not hitherto dared to publish them, alarmed at the fate of our master Copernicus himself who, although he has obtained immortal renown in the eyes of some, yet, in the eyes of a countless host (so great is the number of fools), he appeared as one to be laughed at and hissed off the stage. I would indeed dare to publish my reflections if there were more people like you, but as there are not, I will refrain from affairs of this kind.'

Replying, Kepler regrets Galileo's policy: 'You might, with your doctrine, assist your allies who are struggling against so many adverse judgements; they would draw comfort from your assent and support from your authority. . . . What need is there of deceit? Have faith, Galileo, and go forward. If I judge rightly, few of the leading mathematicians of Europe will wish to hold aloof from us, such power is in the truth.'

To this appeal Galileo returned no reply, and the correspondence between the two men lapsed. Galileo did not openly profess his Copernican faith until he was approaching his fiftieth year, when he first became involved in the controversy through his announcement of his telescopic discoveries. He seems to have been anxious to avoid a breach with his colleagues in the University; and he was, perhaps, influenced by the fate of the Copernican Giordano Bruno, burnt at the stake for manifold heresies in 1600 and of whom no mention is made in Galileo's works. In the meanwhile Galileo's course of instruction in astronomy to elementary students was continued on traditional lines.

Of more momentous import was Kepler's gift of a copy of his 'Mystery' to the illustrious Danish astronomer Tycho Brahe. The chequered friendship that grew out of this literary courtesy proved the most fateful of all the links that Kepler forged with his fellow-mortals. Tycho Brahe (or Tycho, as it has become customary to call him) came of a noble family; he was born in 1546 in what is now southern Sweden but was then a part of Denmark. Early dedicated to the service of the state, he went the round of the principal Protestant Universities; but his youthful interest was turned to astronomy by the occurrence of a solar eclipse on the day foretold for it.

Later, however, the serious discrepancy between the predicted and the observed times of a conjunction of the planets Jupiter and Saturn vividly brought home to him the continuing imprecision of the planetary tables of the period and awakened in him the resolve to undertake the reformation of astronomical science. Returning to Denmark, his education completed, Tycho devoted himself for a space to the pursuit of alchemy. But his attention was recalled to astronomy by the sudden appearance, in November 1572, of one of the most remarkable 'new stars' (temporary stars) on record, which shone forth in the constellation of Cassiopeia and remained for a time visible in broad daylight. Tycho Brahe traced the vicissitudes of the portentous star through the ensuing months; he marshalled and published the observations of it recorded by other European astronomers; and he was one of several observers (Mästlin was another) who succeeded in establishing that the object was farther from the Earth than the Moon is.

It had been the accepted view (following Aristotle) that all such transient outbursts in the night sky (comprising also meteors and comets) arose from the combustion of terrestrial vapours high in the atmosphere but nearer to us than the Moon. But what Tycho and his brother-astronomers had now established for the visitant of 1572, and what they were soon to demonstrate for the great comet of 1577, was that these objects belonged to the celestial regions where physical changes had been deemed impossible. We shall see how Kepler was confronted by just such another 'new' star and how his curiosity, too, was exercised upon the vagaries of comets.

Meanwhile, good fortune took Tycho on a visit to the Landgrave William IV of Hesse, who operated a famous private observatory with a movable roof, and who now commended his guest to the patronage of King Frederick II of Denmark. So in 1576 the monarch placed the young astronomer in possession of the island of Hveen in the Danish Sound and afforded him the means of building and equipping a magnificent observatory. And here, during almost the whole of Kepler's life-span to date, Tycho and his staff of assistants and students had devoted themselves to remedying the greatest deficiency of the planetary astronomy of the age, which was the lack of authentic, refined and systematic observations of the 'planets' (including the Sun and Moon) in all parts of their orbits. The instruments employed were of Tycho's own ingenious design and construction, still, of course, non-telescopic, but superior in precision to any previously or elsewhere available. The observations recorded over all these years were intended by Tycho to provide the basis for a numerically precise scheme of the planetary motions, complete with tables enabling future positions of the planets to be calculated.

Copernicus had attempted to develop his own theory to this point, but with observations barely more numerous than sufficed to determine the constants of the theory, and those observations of very poor quality. Tycho Brahe made no attempt to improve the Copernican theory, for he rejected the motions of the Earth as contrary to Scripture and to sound physics. He devised a planetary theory of his own in which, however, the five planets revolved round the *Sun* while the Sun and Moon revolved round the Earth, supposed stationary at the centre of the Universe. This scheme preserved many of the advantages of the Copernican system (to which, indeed, it could be regarded as mathematically equivalent); and it afforded a convenient half-way house to the conservative or the orthodox who could not bring themselves to go all the way with Copernicus.

However, before he could elaborate his theory, Tycho Brahe lost favour at the Danish court, and it was as an exile sojourning in Germany that he received the gift of Kepler's book. Naturally, Tycho could not accept all Kepler's ideas without reservation; but out of his experience of the many young astronomers who had served him through the years, he formed a favourable opinion of Kepler and addressed an invitation to him. The circumstances of both men had to alter dramatically before the invitation could be accepted.

Meanwhile, Kepler's developing relations with Tycho Brahe were complicated by the disturbing force of a third personality, one Nicholas Reymers Bär, latinized as Ursus, who had risen from obscurity to be Tycho's predecessor in the office of Imperial Mathematician. He had incurred Tycho's unremitting hostility by publishing as his own invention a system of the planets almost identical with that drawn up (but not yet announced) by the Danish astronomer. In principle, this system could be regarded as a switch of the Copernican scheme with the motion of the Earth transferred to the Sun, though Tycho does not seem to have arrived at it in that way. Tycho lashed out with similar accusations of plagiarism against several other scholars. It would not be surprising if two or more astronomers of the period should have independently hit upon the same idea, though Ursus had, in fact, previously visited Tycho's observatory (in the retinue of the alchemist Lange) and had there fallen under suspicion of stealing documents. Now Kepler had written a flattering letter to Ursus, whose commendation he sought for his new book on the 'Cosmographic Mystery'. And Ursus, in making a counter-charge of plagiarism against Tycho Brahe, had used this letter as ammunition in the fight, so that Kepler found himself ranged with Tycho's enemies just when he was most anxious to secure his goodwill. He managed to make his peace with Tycho; but later he found himself burdened with the distasteful task of presenting Tycho's case against Ursus.

In the spring of 1597 Kepler married. His bride was Barbara Müller, the eldest daughter of a prosperous mill-owner, Jobst Müller, who belonged to Gössendorf, not far from Graz. The lady was in her early twenties but had already been twice married and widowed and was the mother of a little girl, Regina, by her first marriage. In the manner of those days, Kepler made her acquaintance by introduction, and he sought her hand in marriage through the good offices of two friends acting as his delegates. The negotiations ran a chequered course, for the prospective father-in-law can have had no high opinion of the suitor's station and prospects in life. On the other hand, considerations of the fortune that his bride would bring to the relief of his own lot seem to have entered distinctly into Kepler's reckoning. Matters were not forwarded by Kepler's seven months' absence in Württemberg during 1596. However, the negotiations were brought to a successful conclusion and the wedding took place on 27 April 1597.

It would have been too much to hope that Kepler's married life would be a very happy one. He was an erratic genius who put his work before all other considerations and for whom his science was a consuming passion like a physical appetite. He was ill advised to marry a woman accustomed to standards of comfort that he would be unable to maintain. In an age when women were excluded from higher education, it was not to be expected that Barbara Kepler would share her husband's ideals or esteem his achievements at their true worth. The flight to Prague in the following year served only to hasten her descent into melancholy and invalidism. Yet enough mutual affection remained to prevent the marriage from breaking up altogether. For the moment, through his wife's family connections with Graz, Kepler was tied to the place for good or evil.

Though Kepler's salary was raised in consideration of his marriage, trouble beset him from several quarters. It started in his home circle with the deaths of his two children, Henry and Susanna, in early infancy. From without came the threat of intensified pressure on the Lutheran community following the accession to power in 1596 of the Archduke Ferdinand, pledged, with the support of the Jesuits, to carry forward the Catholic re-conquest of Styria. Measures of increasing severity were enacted against the Protestants, culminating in the prohibition of their sacraments, the closing of their churches and, eventually, in September 1598, the banishment from Graz, at a day's notice, of all Lutheran teachers and preachers on pain of death. Kepler was forced to share in the hurried exodus; but the order was varied in his case, and he alone was allowed to return a month later. Perhaps his appointment as District Mathematician was held to lie outside the confessional conflict. Or he may have owed his more favourable treatment to his personal moderation in dealing with matters of faith, or to his friendly relations with scientifically minded Jesuits and with the Catholic Chancellor of Bavaria, Herwart von Hohenburg, who corresponded with the astronomer for years on matters of common interest. Meanwhile, he lived on in Graz lacking the ministrations of his Church and in enforced idleness. He explored the possibility of a return to Tübingen; but Mästlin could offer him no encouragement. His hopes turned towards Tycho Brahe, now established at Prague and entering upon his brief career as Mathematician to the Emperor Rudolph II. His invitation to Kepler was cordially renewed late in 1599, and Kepler now felt impelled to visit the Danish astronomer. It was early in January 1600 that he set out for Prague in the retinue of an Imperial emissary. On 4 February he had his first meeting with Tycho Brahe in the castle outside Prague that the Emperor had assigned to his Mathematician.

CHAPTER SEVEN

THE LEGACY OF TYCHO BRAHE

Though only fifty-three years of age, Tycho Brahe felt his powers declining, and he hoped to find in Kepler a vigorous young assistant to help him in sorting out his vast store of observations and in working them up into a set of planetary tables based upon his own conception of the planetary economy. As for Kepler, his immediate need was for data by which to confirm his hypothesis of the regular solids; but he was willing to be cast in the role of an architect destined to supervise the erection of a new structure of astronomy out of all the magnificent building-materials that Tycho had accumulated. Tycho Brahe, so Kepler had declared to Mästlin, 'abounds in riches which, like many rich men, he does not rightly use'. Yet, despite their need of each other, an unbridgeable gulf separated the two astronomers, so strongly contrasted in age, in social origins and standing, in temperament and disposition, and even in their views as to how the planetary system was organized. Each was tormented by his own problems: Tycho was ending his days in exile, the envied favourite of a foreign prince; Kepler, as ever, was dogged by ill-health and hag-ridden by anxiety about what the future held in store for himself and his family. However, he soon took his place among the restless ménage of relatives, assistants and students surrounding the great astronomer, though not without occasional explosions betraying the incompatibility of the two men.

Kepler always saw the hand of Providence ('if God cares about astronomy') in the train of events that, against all the odds, united his fortunes with those of Tycho Brahe. It was a harsh fate that drove the great Danish astronomer into exile almost at the close of his illustrious career. When he sent his first invitation to Kepler, he was living near Hamburg and Kepler was detained by official duties and family cares at Graz, some five hundred miles away. It was only because the German Emperor cared more for astrology and alchemy than for affairs of state, and because the Styrian Jesuits decided to persecute Protestants, that the two incompatible men of genius were set on their collision course and so came to embark upon their brief and stormy but momentous collaboration at Prague. True, when Kepler arrived at the Imperial city, he was disappointed not to find immediately ready to his hand the data he needed to establish his cosmographic scheme. He soon discovered, moreover, that Tycho Brahe was a little hesitant about putting any of his observations at Kepler's disposal except such as were needed for purposes of Tycho's own choosing.

At the moment, the task in hand was that of constructing the orbit of the planet Mars. Tycho's assistant Christen Longberg, called Longomontanus, had been working on this problem but had ceased to make much progress; he was switched to lunar theory and the intractable planet became Kepler's concern. It was thus not along any line of attack of his own choosing that Kepler won through to the central stronghold of planetary theory. It was Tycho Brahe who decided that he should work on the theory of the planet Mars. And here again, in later years, Kepler deemed it providential that he was assigned the one planet (apart from the 'unobservable' Mercury) whose departure from the ideal circular orbit was sufficiently pronounced to be just deducible from observations as accurate as those available. On the other hand, we may account it fortunate that the telescope had not yet been invented and applied to the precise measurement of celestial angles, for then the observed *departures* from Kepler's Laws exhibited by the planets (and due, as we now know, to their mutual gravitational attractions) would have appeared so serious as perhaps to discourage him from formulating the Laws at all.

However, the arduous road ahead was veiled from the young astronomer's sight as he entered upon his appointed task full of confidence; and he laid a bet that he would clear up the Martian problem in a week. However, in order to secure a copy of the planetary observations for his own use, Kepler thought he might have to settle down for a few years as Tycho's assistant, hoping that the political situation at Graz might clarify itself meanwhile.

In June 1600, after spending four months in Prague, Kepler revisited his home in the Styrian capital. He had hoped that the Graz authorities (thanks to some pulling of strings from Prague) would approve his service under Tycho Brahe while continuing to pay him his former stipend as District Mathematician. But it seemed that they were no longer interested in employing him in that capacity; rather they thought that, in such a grave hour, he would be more fittingly occupied as a physician, and they bade him repair to Italy to acquire the requisite qualifications. This development struck at Kepler's tentative plans for returning to Bohemia to work under Tycho Brahe, for he had assumed that he would continue to receive his Graz salary, any additional emoluments from the Imperial treasury being problematic and hard to collect. Still, he would not abandon his astronomical schemes on the eve of success; and he planned to appease the authorities by studying medicine in his spare time. For a moment he even aspired to the visionary office of Mathematician to the Archduke Ferdinand, to whom he addressed an essay on the solar eclipse of 10 July 1600. On that occasion Kepler set up in the marketplace at Graz a crude wooden instrument, later to be described in his optical treatise of 1604 and serving for the more accurate estimation of the extent of an eclipse (the proportion of the Sun's disk covered by the Moon) at any instant during the course of the phenomenon.

Kepler's hopes of entering the service of the Archduke, and, indeed, the basis for his plans for collaborating with Tycho Brahe, were suddenly shattered when Ferdinand summoned all the townsmen of Graz to be examined concerning their religious faith and banished all who were not Catholics. Kepler, maintaining his Protestant profession, was dismissed from his post with six months' pay and given six weeks to leave Graz. The decree was relaxed in his case to the extent of permitting him to lease his wife's houses and lands instead of selling them under compulsion in a buyer's market; and part of the levy on the assets that he took away with him was remitted. On 30 September 1600, within the specified period, Kepler fled from Graz with his wife and his step-daughter Regina. All appeals to Tübingen and Stuttgart were fruitless; Tycho Brahe was now his only refuge. At this crisis, the great Danish astronomer invited the younger man back to Prague with a cordiality that was part of the more generous side of his nature.

Kepler arrived in Prague by way of Linz a sick, broken man with no assured prospects. It was only in later years that he was able to trace the hand of Providence in the tragic vicissitudes that brought him at last to the Bohemian capital and to look back upon the twelve years that he spent there as the most fruitful period of his career when, for a space, he was permitted to practise his faith and his science without suffering persecution. Kepler's wife, too, fell sick in the strange city, cut off from her relatives and reduced to poverty by the high cost of living. The family took up their abode with Tycho Brahe, who was now living in Prague while his instruments, transported from Denmark, were being set up again at a palace outside the city. However, before Kepler could settle to work, he was obliged to revisit Graz to attend to the affairs of his father-in-law, who had lately died. He suffered no interference from the Styrian authorities and benefited from the change.

Barely two months after Kepler's return to Prague an event occurred that was to prove a turning-point in his career, nothing less than the death of his patron Tycho Brahe. The great astronomer was overtaken by sudden illness as he sat eating and drinking at a nobleman's table. Modern surgery could have saved him, but in those days the case was hopeless, and he died on 24 October 1601 at the early age of fifty-four. On his death-bed he bequeathed to Kepler his closely guarded registers of observations and his instruments, but on the understanding that the projected tables of planetary motions—the *Rudolphine Tables*, as they were to be called in honour of the Emperor—should be drawn up in accordance with the Tychonic and not the Copernican planetary theory. The Emperor confirmed Kepler in this inheritance and appointed him to be Imperial Mathematician in succession to Tycho Brahe. However, the deceased astronomer's heirs had still to be reckoned with.

The verdict of history upon the Emperor Rudolph II is that he neglected affairs of state, consorted with grooms, patronized astrologers and alchemists and shut himself up in his palace to busy himself about his vast collections of curiosities and works of art. A confessional conflict already existed

Galileo Galilei

Frontispiece of the *Rudolphine Tables*

in Bohemia, more complicated indeed but scarcely less pronounced than that which disturbed the peace of Styria; but the Emperor cared for none of these things, and his religious indifference operated to Kepler's advantage, so that he was protected from the proselytizing Jesuits. On the other hand, the astronomer was subjected to chronic embarrassment by the irregularity with which his salary was paid, so that he had to subsist largely on whatever he had been able to save out of the wreck of his wife's fortune. The Imperial treasury was depleted to carry on the war against the Turks and to finance the Emperor's extravagant hobbies. One unfortunate consequence was that Kepler could not afford to employ computers to relieve him of the burden of tedious calculations; these occupied time that he could have spent to much greater advantage on theoretical work. In moods of exasperation he even cast about for some other appointment where he could count on the punctual payment of his salary.

Kepler's astronomical interests at this period were not solely theoretical; and though, owing to defective eyesight, he made no claim to be an expert observer of the heavens, yet from time to time his gaze was directed to some arresting celestial spectacle or to some predictable phenomenon from which valuable information might be derived. And although the jealous heirs barred his access no less to Tycho's instruments than to his recorded observations, yet Kepler made some shift to procure instruments of his own. One of his friends, the nobleman with whom he first journeyed to Prague, equipped him with two metal instruments of the kind Tycho had employed; other devices he made for himself of wood. And on occasion Kepler sought to promote some measure of co-operation among his fellow-astronomers, usually so secretive about whatever they had observed. If Kepler was ever in need of skilled mechanical craftsmanship or of technical aids to

computation during his years at Prague, he had only to turn
to Jost Bürgi, a Swiss clockmaker who had begun his career
in the service of the Landgrave William IV of Hesse. It was
the Landgrave who had brought the young Tycho Brahe to
the notice of the Danish King and so launched him upon his
illustrious career. Later, Bürgi entered the Imperial household; there he met Kepler, who benefited from his technical
skill while applying his own theoretical knowledge to the
advantage of the self-taught horologist. Bürgi's invention of
a crude system of logarithms, to which reference is made
elsewhere, affected Kepler very closely because of the immense amount of time he was obliged to spend over trivial
calculations.

In the years following the settlement at Prague, three more
children were born to John and Barbara Kepler—a daughter,
Susanna (second of the name), and two sons, Frederick and
Louis. The roll of god-parents, of noble or ambassadorial
rank, suggests that the astronomer and his family were accepted in the highest social circles and that they managed to
keep up appearances despite financial difficulties that necessi-
tated some harsh economies behind the scenes. Meanwhile,
the family parted with Regina, Kepler's step-daughter, who
married during their residence in Prague. The monotony of
life in the capital was broken for Kepler and his family by
occasional trips on business or to escape from the plague;
these excursions afforded the astronomer excuse for revisiting
his old friends and haunts in Graz and Tübingen.

CHAPTER EIGHT

THE *NEW ASTRONOMY*

We saw how Kepler, on his first visit to Tycho Brahe, was set the task of reducing to a geometrical rule the observed motion of the planet Mars. He lost no time in bringing to bear upon this problem some of the new insights into planetary theory that he had already shared with readers of his *Cosmographic Mystery*. Thus he urged upon Tycho the advantages of referring the planetary motions to the *true* Sun and of making the orbital planes of all the planets pass through that luminary, irrespective of whether the Sun then revolved round the Earth (as Tycho would maintain) or the Earth (numbered by Kepler among the planets) revolved round the Sun. This ensured that each orbital plane maintained a constant inclination to the ecliptic. Again, while both Copernicus and Tycho had insisted upon uniform circular motion for planets, Kepler broke away from this convention and reckoned a planet's angular velocity as uniform, not about the centre of the circular orbit, nor about the Sun, but about some equant point whose position within the orbit remained to be determined. He thus got rid of the last of the planetary epicycles and prepared the way for bringing into action the solar force that he conceived as the physical cause of the planetary motions.

In the early months of his attack upon the theory of Mars, Kepler was hampered by the obligation under which he lay to operate only within the ambit of the Tychonic planetary scheme; and even after Tycho's death he strove to fulfil the terms of the bargain under which he enjoyed access to the great astronomer's registers. But the compulsive logic of his own discoveries soon left him no freedom of choice between the rival cosmological systems and even forced him to abandon belief in any kind of circular planetary orbit. Kepler's long, agonizing quest went on into the years following Tycho's death. He described its course in letters to brother-astronomers, but above all in the pages of his greatest book, justly entitled the *New Astronomy*. This is not a treatise, a systematic presentation of results, but a testament, the record of an almost spiritual pilgrimage, conducting the reader along all the windings of the road (and up all its blind alleys) and recording the play of the great astronomer's passing moods. With its intricate calculations and speculative flights of fancy, the *New Astronomy* is the most difficult to read of all the half-dozen decisive cosmological books of the world, and the more so as its author was wrestling for much of the time with mathematical problems requiring for their rigorous and elegant solution concepts and notations not at that period available. Yet some account must be attempted of the historic advances in planetary theory that the book records.

Of the five Parts into which the *New Astronomy* is divided, the first establishes that the Ptolemaic, the Copernican and the Tychonic systems were all equally well able to represent *mathematically* the apparent motions of the Sun, Moon and planets, physical considerations apart. Here, too, is stressed the cardinal role of the true Sun. In Part II Kepler sets out his hypothetical circular orbit of Mars and proceeds to determine the geometrical *elements* of the orbit—the eccentricity, or proportional displacement of the Sun S from the centre C (Fig. 6), the direction of the line joining the apses A and B, where

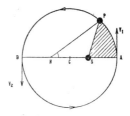

6. Kepler's Hypothetical Circular Orbit
for Mars

the planet is respectively nearest to and farthest from the Sun,
and the position of the equant point H (he eventually found
that setting off CH equal to CS gave the best results). These
elements were to be determined from sets of four of Tycho's
observations of Mars in opposition, when the true Sun, the
Earth and the planet lay roughly in a straight line. At such
times a planet appears to us to lie in the same direction as if
we were viewing it from the Sun, and uncertainties about the
elements of the Earth's orbit do not affect the result. By a
tedious trial-and-error procedure, involving some seventy
trials, Kepler arrived at an orbit that fitted a selection of the
available opposition observations to within two minutes of
arc (which represents about the limit of certainty of the normal
eye's judgement of direction). But when he tested his orbit by
reference to other opposition observations of the planet, the
discrepancies could amount to eight minutes of arc (or about
a quarter of the angular breadth of the full moon); and Kepler
felt certain that Tycho's observations could not have been out
by this amount. 'Since the Divine Goodness has granted us
Tycho Brahe (he writes), that most diligent observer, from
whose observations an error in this Ptolemaic calculation of
eight minutes in the position of Mars has been proved, it is
right that with grateful hearts we should both acknowledge
and put to use this gift of God. . . . These eight minutes alone
have pointed the way to the reformation of the whole of
astronomy.'

So in Part III Kepler turned aside to investigate the annual motion of the *Earth*, the moving platform from which all our celestial observations have to be made. He had about reached this stage when Tycho Brahe died. Copernicus had assumed that the Earth sped round its orbit at a uniform speed; but Kepler was convinced that the Earth's orbit would be found to possess an equant just like that of any other planet. This was no mere argument from analogy; it was based upon the physical considerations that had long been taking shape in Kepler's mind. By ingeniously selecting a set of observations of Mars with the planet always at roughly the same point on its orbit but the Earth variously situated, he was able to pinpoint the corresponding positions of the Earth and hence to determine the elements of its orbit. He had been right in his surmise: the Earth revolved uniformly round an equant point equidistant with the Sun from the centre of the Earth's eccentric orbit.

Like most of his contemporaries, Kepler accepted Aristotle's dictum that force is needed to keep a body moving and that the speed of the body is proportional to the force applied to it. It was in conformity to this principle that he now tried to explain a planet's motion as caused by a force somehow applied to it by the Sun and acting in the direction of motion, along the tangent of the orbit. The periods of revolution of the successive planets increase as we pass out from the Sun, but in a greater ratio than the circumferences of their orbits; and this suggested that the force emanating from the Sun became weaker with increasing distance from the luminary. It was natural to assume tentatively that this force varied in inverse proportion to the distance.

Now when Kepler had established that Mars and the Earth revolved uniformly with respect to equant points symmetrically situated in relation to the Sun, he felt confirmed in his momentous decision to introduce physical considerations into the context of the planetary problem. For the location of the equant point implied that, even within a single orbit, the planet moved faster or slower according to its nearness to or distance from the Sun. And at the two apses, at least, where the planet is moving at right angles to the direction of the Sun, its speed *is* inversely as its distance from the Sun. For if v_1 and v_2 are the speeds at the respective apses A and B (Fig. 6), then, since CS = CH, we have HA = SB, HB = SA, and (by the definition of an equant)

$$\frac{v_1}{HA} = \frac{v_2}{HB}.$$

We have then

$$\frac{v_1}{v_2} = \frac{HA}{HB} = \frac{SB}{SA}$$

which establishes the law of the inverse distance for the apses A and B.

Kepler now made the working assumption that this law held good *all round* the Earth's orbit, which represented a definite departure from the hypothesis of the equant point. It implied that the *time* required for the Earth to traverse a short arc of its orbit at P, say, must be directly proportional to its *distance* SP from the Sun. Hence the time required for the Earth to traverse a considerable arc must be as the *sum* of all the distances drawn to all the short arcs into which it could be broken up. Actually, Kepler divided the Earth's circular orbit into 360 equal parts and computed the distance from the Sun to each point of division. The test of his hypothesis was that the sum of the distances between A and P should stand in the same proportion to the sum of *all* the distances as the time from A to P stood to the length of the year. The idea that a plane surface was made up of a multitude of lines was not then so unacceptable to mathematicians as it afterwards became. It was only a short step to regard the time from A to P as proportional to the *area* ASP swept out by the radius vector SP and easily calculable for the circle, though at the moment Kepler regarded this rule only as a convenient but inexact substitute for the summation of distances. Any of the three hypotheses—the equant, the summation of distances, the description of areas—gave satisfactory results for the Earth's orbit because of its relatively small eccentricity. In the light of later-established dynamical principles it was the last of these three hypotheses, the 'area law', with its mathematical inelegancies smoothed out, that has been generalized and adopted as Kepler's 'second Law of Planetary Motion': 'The radius vector joining the Sun to a planet sweeps out equal areas in equal times.'

Kepler now (Part IV) reversed the procedure he had adopted for determining the Earth's orbit: he chose observations with the Earth always in the same place and pinpointed the corresponding positions of Mars so as to determine the elements of its orbit. But at this point the tools of the antique astronomy broke in his hands. He found that, if he assigned to Mars an eccentric orbit of a size to fit the planet's distances from the Sun when near the apses, then, at other parts of the orbit, Mars lay not on but within the circle so that it appeared to revolve in some sort of egg-shaped curve. At this point Kepler's progress seems to have been arrested, partly by difficulties arising out of a dispute with the heirs of Tycho Brahe concerning rights of access to the dead astronomer's observations, partly out of his researches in the closely related field of optics which occupied much of the year 1602 and the whole of 1603 and culminated in the publication of his massive optical treatise, the *Supplement to Witelo*, in 1604. It was after Kepler's return to the problem of Mars that some of his most agonizing struggles occurred. He dramatized them under the metaphor of a military operation undertaken against the grim old god of war himself whose name the planet bears and whose effigy figures on the diagram exhibiting the solution of the planetary problem (Fig. 7).

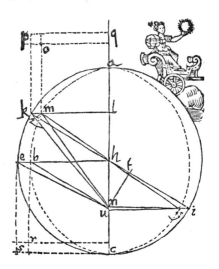

7. Kepler's Solution of the Problem of Mars

By the end of 1604 Kepler had become convinced that the hypothesis of an oval orbit for Mars was misconceived. He did not then suspect an elliptic orbit (the simplest kind of oval); that would have simplified the problem, since Apollonius of Perga had long since explored the properties of the ellipse. At Christmas 1604, ill and dispirited, he drew up a report of his researches thus far for the Emperor's information (it covered Chapters 1 to 51 of the *New Astronomy*) and he approached Mästlin and the Tübingen authorities with proposals for publication in case he died before bringing the work to a satisfactory conclusion. However, soon after Easter 1605 a chance observation of the equality of two numbers in his calculations suggested a mathematical relation that he recognized as holding only for the ellipse; and thus he was led at last to his 'first Law of Planetary Motion' (initially established only for Mars), that a planet describes an elliptic orbit with the Sun occupying one of the two foci.

Rather surprisingly, Kepler was slow to recognize the mathematical properties of the ellipse when they revealed themselves in the orbit he was fitting to Mars. The geometry of the conic sections had been worked out very thoroughly in antiquity, as we saw, but not in the trigonometrical terms appropriate here. Kepler was not primarily a mathematician; and he showed but little interest in considerations of pure geometry except when they arose as side-issues to concrete problems such as fitting the regular solids to the planetary spheres, or, as here, providing a planet with a definable orbit, or, in later years, gauging the capacity of wine casks.

Kepler finished his *New Astronomy* in 1605 except for Part V (dealing with the motions of the planets in latitude), which was added in 1606. Publication was delayed until 1609, largely in consequence of Kepler's dispute with the heirs of Tycho Brahe. Upon the Danish astronomer's death, the Emperor appointed Kepler to succeed to the office of Imperial Mathematician and directed him to carry on with the researches in which the two astronomers had been jointly engaged. At the same time, Rudolph came to a financial agreement with the heirs over Kepler's continued use of Tycho's observations. However, the situation was not quite so simple: Kepler was, in fact, developing on his own initiative a planetary theory that ran counter to Tycho's deepest convictions and yet depended at every turn upon his observations. Opposition to this arrangement came chiefly from Franz Tengnagel, a Westphalian nobleman, Tycho's son-in-law, who adopted rather a dog-in-the-manger attitude over the observations. He revived a plan of Tycho's for publishing a set of planetary tables.

Kepler maintained that the reformation of planetary theory should be completed first; but, in return for continued access to the observations, he had to agree not to publish his theory until Tengnagel had finished his tables, which he was in no hurry to do. Later, Tengnagel wanted changes made in the text of the *New Astronomy*, to which Kepler would not agree. Eventually the dispute was resolved on the condition that Kepler's book should include a short (and not unfriendly) foreword by Tengnagel warning the reader not to be misled by the freedom with which Kepler had departed from the views of Tycho Brahe, particularly in some of his physical discussions, and stressing the dependence of the whole work upon the observational foundations laid by the Danish astronomer. Another obstacle to publication was the cost of printing the book at a time when the Imperial finances were straitened. Kepler received a grant in 1607 and started printing; but the *New Astronomy* did not appear for another two years. The Emperor kept the marketing of the book in his own hands and would not even allow Kepler the usual complimentary copies to present to his friends and to distinguished personages.

The *New Astronomy* lay rather beyond the grasp of Kepler's contemporaries, and in any case the underlying Copernican doctrine was not widely accepted. Even Kepler's faithful correspondents were mystified. Moreover, the book was printed only in a limited edition. For all these reasons its appearance excited relatively little interest.

CHAPTER NINE

FIRST STEPS IN CELESTIAL MECHANICS

Not the least significant part of the *New Astronomy* is its Introduction, in which Kepler criticized the traditional views on terrestrial gravity and on the agencies that keep the planets moving in their orbits. The distinction he was compelled to draw between these two topics is itself instructive. Before the century was out, gravity was to be generalized into a universal force between bodies, operating, indeed, to determine the fall of heavy objects on the Earth, but equally constraining a planet already endowed with motion to keep to a closed orbit instead of travelling off into space along a tangent. But Kepler never escaped from mechanical ideas going back to Aristotle and seemingly consistent with common experience. He believed that a body would come to rest if it were not continuously impelled by a force. He employed, indeed, the word *inertia*; but it meant for him this sluggish quality of matter, not, as it does for us, the tendency of a body to continue in its existing state, whether of rest or of motion. So, though he conceived both gravity and the Sun's action on a planet as in some sense 'magnetic', he could never identify them. For he supposed that the force needed to keep the planet moving must act *tangentially* along its orbit, while gravity draws a heavy object in *radially* towards the attracting body; and there seemed no possibility of unifying these two agencies.

However, it was Kepler who took the first steps towards the modern, purely mechanical conception of planetary motion. He insisted that the centre about which a body revolved, or the goal which it strove to reach, must itself be a *body*; it could not be a mere empty point in space. This principle, clearly grasped in the 'Mystery' of 1596, was developed in the *New Astronomy* in relation to Kepler's doctrine of gravity. 'A mathematical point (he writes), whether it be the centre of the Universe or not, cannot make heavy bodies approach itself. ... Let physicists prove if they can that natural objects have a sympathy with that which is *nothing*. ... The true doctrine of gravity rests upon the following axioms: Every corporeal substance, as such, tends by nature to rest in the place where it is while outside the sphere of force of a cognate body. Gravity consists in a mutual corporeal affection between cognate bodies towards their union or connection (the magnetic property is also of this order), so that the Earth attracts a stone much more than the stone seeks the Earth.'

This passage reveals the influence of William Gilbert's book on magnetism, with which Kepler must have become acquainted soon after its publication in 1600 and of which he formed a very high opinion. However, at this stage, Kepler may have had no precise magnetic mechanism in mind, only a vague analogy between magnetic and gravitational attractions.

Heavy bodies, in Kepler's view, did not seek the centre of the Earth as such; they sought to join themselves to the Earth as to a cognate body. If their courses appeared to converge upon the centre, that was merely an effect of symmetry, the Earth being a sphere. 'If two stones were placed in any given part of the Universe, near to each other and outside the sphere of force of a third, cognate body, then the two stones, like two magnetic bodies, would unite at some intermediate point, each approaching the other through a distance proportional to the mass (*moles*) of the other. Were the Earth and the Moon not held each in its orbit through a spiritual, or other such equivalent force, the Earth would rise towards the Moon through a fifty-fourth part of the distance between them, and the Moon would descend towards the Earth through the other fifty-three parts [assuming the sizes of the Earth and the Moon to be as fifty-three to one and their densities to be equal]. If the Earth ceased to draw the waters to itself, all the water of the sea would be caught up and would flow to the Moon. The sphere of the Moon's attraction extends to the Earth and draws up the water in the torrid zone.' Thus the tides arise, as Kepler proceeds to explain, though this view of their causation did not originate with him. Kepler continues: 'If the Moon's attractive force extends as far as the Earth, much more must the Earth's attractive force extend as far as the Moon, and far beyond; moreover, nothing consisting in any wise of earthly material, caught up on high, can escape from the powerful hold of this attraction.'

Gravity was thus exalted into an agency operating between cosmic bodies. For the moment, however, it was restricted to the Earth and the Moon. These bodies were widely regarded at that period (in particular, by Mästlin) as sharing a common nature. They were still marked off from the other heavenly bodies, and particularly from the Sun, which occupied a unique central place in the Universe of Kepler.

Besides being a *goal* of motion (under gravity), the Earth is also a *centre* of motion, for the Moon circulates round it, as Kepler had pointed out already in Chapter 16 of his *Cosmographic Mystery* of 1596: '. . . And indeed the Creator, in His love for men, appears to have clothed the Earth with this last, lunar orbit because He desired to confer upon her a status similar to that of the Sun. For if the Earth, too, were the centre of some orbit (as the Sun is the centre of them all), she could be regarded as like a Sun of sorts; on which account she has been generally taken to be the common centre of the entire Universe.'

However, the central body *par excellence* is the Sun; and in both the *Cosmographic Mystery* and the *New Astronomy* Kepler tries to explain, in various ways, how the Sun may act upon a planet. To quote again from the Introduction to the latter work: 'The Sun remains in its place, but it rotates as if upon a turning-lathe and sends out from itself into the depths of the Universe an immaterial species of its body analogous to the immaterial species of its light. This species turns with the rotation of the Sun after the manner of a most rapid whirlpool throughout the whole extent of the Universe, and it bears the planets along with it in a circle with a stronger or a weaker thrust according as, by the law of its emanation, it is denser or rarer.' The term *species*, as we have seen, carried overtones of medieval philosophy, and it had come to be applied to light. However, the solar species could not be identified with light, or the Earth would stop moving whenever the Sun's rays were cut off from it at a time of solar eclipse.

Kepler regarded the motion of a planet as a sort of compromise between the motive power of the Sun and the natural 'inertia' of matter. In order to follow its appointed course, a planet had no need of intelligence, only of an instinct such as determines what manner of flowers and how many leaves a plant shall bear. When, however, some ten years later, Kepler came to write his *Epitome of Copernican Astronomy*, he sought to account, on purely mechanical principles, for the fluctuation in a planet's distance from the Sun consequent upon its elliptic orbit. By that time, too, it had been established, following Galileo's telescopic observations, that the Sun did indeed rotate on its axis, a discovery that Kepler had had to anticipate in faith in order to be able to explain the planetary motions in the way that he did.

CHAPTER TEN

THE PHILOSOPHY OF ASTROLOGY

Early in his career, while still a student, Kepler had come to embrace the view, shared alike by learned and simple folk in his time, that the fortunes of human life were bound up with the vicissitudes of the heavenly bodies. Astrology survives to this day in some quarters as a popular superstition; in Kepler's time it still cemented the structure and pervaded the discourse of natural philosophy and medicine to much the same extent as the established principles of conservation of energy and the like are basic to the physical science of our modern age.

It is tempting to adopt a superior attitude towards these old-world thinkers and to regard it as a detraction even from Kepler's fame that he, too, should have shared the common delusion. However, it is only through centuries of scientific discipline that we have acquired a fair ability to look in the right direction for the 'cause' of any unfamiliar phenomenon that we wish to 'explain'. The early thinkers were completely at sea when confronted with such a problem. And we should rather commend their high endeavour in seeking for order and meaning behind the phantasmagoria of experience than ridicule them for postulating causal connections between phenomena that we now judge to be totally unrelated. Whatever we may think of it, astrological ideas figured so prominently in Kepler's mature thoughts and writings that some account of the origins and precepts of the pseudo-science seems to be called for at this point.

It was formerly believed that scientific astronomy grew out of astrology. However that may be, astrology, or at least the astrological tradition that the West inherited, appears to have developed in the Mediterranean lands from the widespread worship of 'the host of heaven', the planets being associated or identified with the principal gods of the Babylonian pantheon or conceived as seasonal aspects of the supreme Sungod. Celestial, or often merely atmospheric phenomena were treated as portents, at first of the fate of kings or nations, later (under the more settled conditions of the great empires), of private individuals. Complicated systems of prognostication were constructed and propagated through the ancient world.

The Greeks remained singularly free from the prevailing obsession until their colonists, following the conquests of Alexander the Great, came into close contact with the Middle Eastern peoples. Meanwhile, however, the Greek philosophers had been unwittingly preparing the way for the subsequent permeation of Mediterranean civilization by oriental astrology. They had established the conception of ineluctable natural laws; and submission to these laws had become a Stoic virtue. Plato had given life to the stars and had assigned one to each human soul. Aristotle was not astrologically given; but he had made physical changes on the Earth proceed from motions in the heavens. The planets, whose Greek names had formerly been mere descriptive adjectives, had begun to be called after the gods. 'The Orontes flowed into the Tiber'; astrology and sorcery flourished in the Rome of the Caesars, despite Imperial proscriptions; it formed the theme of a long poem by Manilius (edited by a much more accomplished

Latin versifier, A. E. Housman); even Ptolemy, the prince of ancient astronomers, was as celebrated in the Middle Ages for his astrological as for his astronomical writings.

Already in pagan times the determinism of astrology had been condemned by moral philosophers as incompatible with the full responsibility of men for their actions. In Christian circles these objections carried even more weight. Yet the medieval Church continued to admit at least 'natural' astrology, finding support in the obvious connections between terrestrial events and the celestial routine (such as the dependence of the tides upon the lunar cycle). More ambitious systems of prognostication could be rendered morally harmless by adopting the view that the stars merely showed what was likely to happen so that steps could be taken to ensure that it did not. Or the planetary phenomena could be regarded as the divinely appointed *signs*, and not the *causes* of the calamities that were about to plague humanity. Throughout the Middle Ages astrology (reinforced in due course by a vigorous Muslim tradition) dominated chemistry, mineralogy, anatomy and medicine in virtue of the sympathy supposed to subsist between the planets and the elements and qualities of the sublunary realm, or the organs and humours of the body. The Renaissance, through its preoccupation with classical studies, stimulated interest in astrology; and the Reformation did little to check it. So we must not be surprised to find Kepler yielding to the importunity of friends and patrons and furnishing them with the horoscopes for which they made request. Kepler occasionally likens astronomy and astrology to a mother and her daughter. Wise mother Astronomy would go hungry if not supported and nourished by foolish daughter Astrology and her ditties. Or (reversing the relationship) daughter Astronomy cannot disown her mother and nurse, Astrology.

Long before Kepler's time the technique of horoscopic astrology had become well established. The standard procedure consisted in dividing the zodiac into twelve equal portions (*houses*), reckoning from the point of the ecliptic (the *ascendant*) that was just rising above the horizon when the critical event (e.g. the birth of a child) took place. These houses (to be distinguished from the signs of the zodiac) were numbered from one to twelve in the order East, North, West, South; the horoscopic diagram was commonly drawn as a square instead of a circle (Fig. 8 shows the horoscope of Albrecht Wallenstein to which further reference will be made

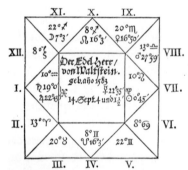

8. The Horoscope of Wallenstein

in the sequel). Each house corresponded to some phase of the life of the person (the *querent*) whose destiny was being sought. Information about his fate was to be elicited by noting which planets were in the various houses; which signs of the zodiac the various planets occupied; whether a planet was in one of the signs peculiarly its own, and whether it was situated at the degree of the ecliptic where it was deemed to exert its greatest influence (in its *exaltation*). Much depended also upon whether two planets were in the same house or sign (in *conjunction*), or were separated in the sky by some simple sub-multiple of 360° (defining their *aspect*).

Calculating nativities represented for Kepler an additional source of income. Yet he could never undertake these geneth-liac exercises with a quiet conviction of their validity. His attitude to the astrological doctrine and practice of his day was sceptical and ambivalent; and he kept trying to clarify his ideas on the subject. Indeed, the first book he published after his migration to Prague, *On the Surer Foundations of Astrology*, was an astrological confession of faith embodying a forecast for the year 1602. It consists of seventy-five theses written in Latin as being addressed to the learned in an effort to purify astrology for the common good. Kepler had been confirmed in his cautious acceptance of astrology by Tycho Brahe (who thought the five planets must have been created for *some* purpose since the Sun and Moon sufficed for timekeeping); and the book appeared immediately after Tycho's death, dedi-cated to the nobleman at whose table the Danish astronomer had sat feasting when he was overtaken by his fatal illness.

Kepler's was a 'natural' astrology that conceived the Uni-verse as an animated whole with man centrally situated and receptive of all the cosmic influences descending upon him in the rays of the heavenly bodies. He was concerned in his little book with the operation of these influences, classified as partly physical, partly geometrical. The physical influences involved the four Aristotelian qualities—the hot, the cold, the dry, the moist—from the union of which in compatible pairs the four elements—fire, air, water, earth—were compounded. But while Aristotle had admitted only the *presence* or the *absence* of these qualities, Kepler characteristically laid stress upon the *degree* (of excess, mediocrity or deficiency) of heat and moisture. (Cold and dryness were merely the *absence* of qualities and could exert no positive influence.) The Sun supplied a moderate warmth which undoubtedly varied with the cycle governing the length of the day. The Moon exerted a moistening power; bodies containing moisture swelled with the waxing, shrank with the waning Moon; the tides obviously followed the lunar cycle. For the rest, Kepler satisfied himself that only five essentially different combinations of degrees of warmth and moisture were possible. These he respectively assigned to the five planets, which differed correspondingly in colour according to the nature of their surfaces and their capacities for reflecting the Sun's rays. The planets generate nothing on the Earth; their role is strictly instrumental.

Turning now to the geometrical influences: astrologers attached especial significance (as we have seen) to the *aspect*, or situation of one planet with respect to another, particularly when the two planets appeared close together in the sky or were separated by arcs (of 60°, 90°, 120°, 180°) that were simple fractions of a complete circumference, making five aspects in all. Kepler regarded these aspects as 'nobler' than physical agencies, and he added three to their number, corresponding to angles (of 72°, 135°, 144°) that, like the others, can be constructed with ruler and compasses. He was to take up this subject again in his 'Harmony' of 1619. He seems to have regarded the Earth as possessing some innate capacity for apprehending these regular configurations of the planets in some such way as a plant unreflectingly observes numerical rules in its growth (forming, for instance, a certain invariable number of petals), or as one musically untrained appreciates music. The virtue of the aspects resides not in the planets but in the angles separating them in the sky.

CHAPTER ELEVEN

THOUGHTS ON LIGHT

In the thick of his struggle with the problem of Mars, Kepler found time to take up the study of the properties of light. These parallel interests were, after all, closely related, for the astronomer is much concerned with the phenomena of light, and the more so as his instruments become increasingly elaborate and his standards of precision more refined. Before Tycho Brahe's observations could provide the basis for Kepler's improved planetary theory, they required to be corrected for the refraction which rays of light suffer in passing through the Earth's atmosphere on their way from some celestial body to the observer's eye. Tycho, indeed, had drawn up tables of corrections for the effects of this phenomenon. But he had wrongly supposed that the light of the Sun, the Moon and the stars suffered different degrees of refraction, necessitating the preparation of three separate tables; and he was under the false impression that refraction ceases altogether when a certain elevation above the horizon is reached. So this unsolved problem pressed on Kepler; and the first of his two great optical treatises was centred upon the urgent problem of atmospheric refraction, just as the second was to be called forth by the necessity of explaining precisely how the newly invented telescope worked. If these two optical classics have never ranked with the *New Astronomy*, it is because the exact

law of refraction escaped Kepler as it had escaped his pre-
decessors.

The scientific approach to the problems of light and vision
did not begin with Kepler. The Greeks were early caught by
the fascination of light, and they speculated on the mysterious
process by which we 'see' the world around us. Did feeling
rays emanate from the eye and lay hold of neighbouring
objects or meet with other rays coming from these? Or did
bodies continually shoot off thin films and so impress their
image on the eye? Or was 'pellucidity', the capacity to be
seen through, just a property of the all-pervading medium?
However that might be, the Greeks soon brought their geometry to bear upon the phenomena of light, introducing the
fruitful concept of the *ray* of light which emanates from a
luminous source and suffers various vicissitudes. This ancient
tradition was taken up and greatly enriched by the Muslim
physicist Ibn al-Haitham, called Alhazen; his *Optics*, written
about A.D. 1000 and translated into Latin, was extensively
drawn upon, in its turn, by the Polish optician Witelo, called
Vitellio, whose *Perspective*, dating from about 1270, contained
all that was then known about the science in western Christendom. Both these books were edited by Frederick Risner in
his *Treasury of Optics* of 1572. Kepler possessed a copy of this
collection; and when he came to write on light he took
Witelo's manual as a sort of text. But he built on to it a
treatise on astronomical optics; and the composite nature of
his book is shown by its double title, *Supplement to Witelo,
giving the Optical Part of Astronomy*.

The germ of the book was a discovery that Kepler made
about the so-called 'pin-hole camera', which was employed
in those days for observing solar eclipses. Light from the
partially obscured Sun was admitted through a small hole
into a dark room where it formed an inverted image of the

spectacle upon a screen. Viewed in this way, the Moon, always new at the time of a solar eclipse, looked smaller than it did when full. Tycho Brahe thought that the Moon might really suffer a fluctuation in size as it passed through its phases; but Kepler arrived at the true optical explanation. The image of the Sun is enlarged every way by an amount equal to the radius of the opening through which the light is admitted; it thus encroaches upon the image of the eclipsing Moon and makes this look smaller. It was this discovery that Kepler wanted to publish as a sort of appendix to Witelo; in the event he was led on to produce a comprehensive treatise on light.

The book begins with some general considerations on the nature of light. Kepler conceived light as one of the cosmic forces serving to fashion and to animate the Universe and to enable bodies to act upon one another. It is non-material, but it possesses a certain substantiality and is subject to geometrical laws. From each point of a luminous surface light streams out in all directions. It travels in straight lines and moves at an infinite speed, since, being weightless, it offers no resistance to the force that impels it. Light spreads out like the surface of an expanding sphere. It is indestructible; but the greater the area over which it is distributed, the weaker the illumination, which thus varies inversely as the square of the distance from the source: this physical law, here grasped intuitively by Kepler, was established in the eighteenth century by photometric experiments. Conceived thus as a surface, light can be influenced only by falling upon and illuminating another surface, the boundary of a different medium, where it is partly reflected, partly refracted (if the medium is transparent) and partly absorbed. Light acquires a coloration in passing through a dense medium; it is accompanied by heating effects; it destroys or bleaches materials upon which it falls.

There follows the theory of the pin-hole camera, with the solution of the eclipse mystery already referred to, and an explanation of why the image which the camera forms of the uneclipsed Sun is always circular, whatever the shape of the aperture through which the light is admitted. Next come the definition of, and the rule for locating, the image of a luminous source formed by reflection or refraction. The law of reflection, the equality of the angles of the incident and the reflected rays with the normal to the point of incidence, had been known since antiquity and could be explained in quasi-mechanical terms. But the law of refraction was another matter.

Ptolemy the astronomer tabulated, and claimed to have measured, the refraction suffered by a light-ray at the interface of two transparent media; but his figures appear to have been calculated from a formula. An instrument for measuring the refraction of light into water or glass was described, and the results tabulated, by Alhazen and Witelo, who were aware that the angle of refraction was not simply proportional to the angle of incidence. Kepler, as was his way, leads the reader through all the intricacies of his search for a general relation between corresponding angles of incidence and refraction. The now-accepted law, discovered in Kepler's lifetime by Willebrord Snell but first published, by Descartes, seven years after the astronomer's death, states that, for refraction from any one given medium to another, the sine of the angle of incidence (i) is proportional to the sine of the angle of refraction (r):

$$\frac{\sin i}{\sin r} = \text{a constant depending upon the media involved.}$$

The nearest approach Kepler could make to this law, after many experiments, seems to have been a relation of the form

$$i - r = C.i.\sec r,$$

where C is a constant; this gives fairly good agreement with Witelo's refraction table for air and water.

Kepler tried to formulate corrections for atmospheric refraction; but he could proceed only by treating the atmosphere as a layer of incompressible fluid whose height had to be determined and was thought to be less than that of the highest mountains. Yet his refraction tables marked an improvement upon those of Tycho Brahe. In the course of these efforts he tried to make use of the properties of a parabolic curve. He was thus led on to discuss the whole class of the 'conic sections', of which the parabola is a member; and he recognized that these curves can be arranged in an unbroken sequence in which we pass from the circle through the ellipse, parabola and hyperbola to the straight line. One historic consequence of this involvement of the conics in an optical context was the introduction into geometry of the word 'focus', which Kepler had employed to signify the 'hearth' or meeting-point of the rays of light.

An important chapter of Kepler's book is that dealing with vision. The anatomical textbooks of his day gave a generally correct account of the structure of the eye; but it was reserved for him to clear up the prevailing confusion as to the functions of its various parts and to explain the process of seeing in physiological terms. His presentation of the organ of sight as an optical instrument has required only minor amendments from later investigators. He grasped the essential role of the eye, which is to produce an image of the visible scene upon the retina. The pupil was too large to serve as a pin-hole camera; but the cornea, or convex front of the eye, acting like a lens, caused the beam of light passing through it to converge towards a focus behind the retina. It suffered a further refraction at the back surface of the crystalline lens upon passing into the vitreous humour (which is situated between the lens and the retina), and so came to a focus *on* the retina. Experiments on the refraction of light through a globular flask full of water showed that the beam did not come to a sharp point-focus. Kepler concluded that the refracting surface of the crystalline lens must be hyperboloidal rather than spherical so as to obviate this phenomenon; he was unaware of the complex internal structure of the lens and of other factors minimizing 'spherical aberration' within the eye.

Kepler's views on the working of the eye conflicted with those of Alhazen and (following him) of Witelo, who held that the crystalline lens was the essential organ of sight. They thought that the optic nerve, originating from the front of the brain and spreading out funnel-wise, was directly connected with the circumference of the lens, to which it conveyed a subtle fluid giving the lens the power to perceive and to convey the visible form to the nerve by refraction through the vitreous humour.

It might have been expected that only objects situated at a certain fixed distance from the eye would form a sharp image on the retina and be clearly seen; but in fact we enjoy distinct vision of everything lying within a great range of distances. Kepler entertained two alternative explanations of the eye's power of *accommodation*: either the distance between lens and retina suffered an appropriate adjustment, or the density of the vitreous humour was suitably modified; in one way or the other the formation of a sharp image was ensured. It remained for later physiologists to refer accommodation to changes in the convexity of the crystalline lens and in the aperture of the pupil. Meanwhile, Kepler was able to explain the use of spectacle lenses to correct the common defects of vision. It may be that the contemporary optician Maurolycus shared, but published too late to influence, Kepler's sounder ideas on the functions of the eye and the properties of the pin-hole camera.

The second, astronomical part of Kepler's treatise deals, first, with the generation and the reception of light by celestial bodies, and next, with parallax, the apparent change in position of these bodies that results from the displacement of the observer. The two themes converge in the theory of eclipses, which forms the culminating point of the treatise. Much could be learnt from eclipses in Kepler's day; in fact, he called them 'the astronomer's eyes'. The prediction and observation of these phenomena served to test the accuracy of the tables claiming to give the positions of the Sun and Moon in the sky at any stated time. Moreover, eclipses served as 'celestial signals' for the determination of longitude. Two widely separated observers would record, each in his local time, the instant when a solar eclipse began or finished; the difference of the times then indicated the difference of the longitudes of the two observers.

Kepler has something to say about physical astronomy. The Sun, the source of light and warmth and of the motive power impelling the planets in their courses, derives its heat not from combustion but from a vital faculty such as living creatures possess. Equalling in mass all the other heavenly bodies put together, the Sun is composed of a clear, transparent fluid of such immense density that only rays of light reaching the solar surface perpendicularly emerge from it; the rest suffer total internal reflection. Hence, most of the Sun's light reaching us comes from its centre. Kepler says elsewhere that the Sun's light comes to us 'in no time'; also, that the heavens are invisible, the air being the blue sphere that we call the sky. Already, anticipating Galileo, Kepler shared the view of his master Mästlin, and, indeed, of Plutarch, that the Moon's surface was rather like that of the Earth, with mountains and seas and inhabitants. The planets must be self-luminous; otherwise Venus would exhibit phases like the Moon (Galileo was soon to show that it does). Comets were illuminated by the Sun; their tails were probably due to light refracted through their globular, glassy heads and falling on material floating in the aether. Kepler correctly explained the dim luminosity of the Moon when totally eclipsed as due to light refracted by our atmosphere into the Earth's shadow. He thought the phenomenon might serve for investigating the refractive power of the atmospheric air and any local variations to which it might be subject.

Some confusion still existed about the reason why solar eclipses are sometimes *total* (the Moon completely covering the Sun) and sometimes *annular* (an uneclipsed ring of the Sun appearing round the Moon's disk). The distinction arises from variations in the relative distances of Sun and Moon from the Earth; but Tycho Brahe (who was disposed to deny the possibility of total solar eclipses) suggested a pulsation of the Moon, periodically altering its size, while Kepler explained the annular phenomenon as due to the illumination of a lunar atmosphere. He regarded parallax as a God-given aid to the discovery of the structure and scale of the Universe. Our two eyes, set at a certain distance apart and seeing an object in slightly different directions and aspects, serve for the estimation of distances on a small scale. For objects at cosmic distances the effective separation of the eyes can be widened by simultaneously observing from different stations on the Earth, or, if simultaneity cannot be established, by observing a heavenly body from a known station and calculating its direction as seen from the centre of the Earth. Parallax resulting from an annual revolution of the Earth round the Sun should enable distances to be estimated far into the depths of space, a prophecy of what has since come to pass.

Kepler presented the manuscript of his 'Supplement to Witelo' to the Emperor on the first day of 1604, and it was published in the autumn of that year. The publication was hastened in order that the book might embody an appeal to astronomers to direct their attention to the forthcoming solar eclipse of 12 October 1605, which was admirably circumstanced for observation in Europe. Kepler urged the importance of the eclipse as affording precise information about the shape of the Moon's orbit and the intricacies of her apparent motion through the heavens. What he had learnt about the Moon's behaviour during his first visit to Tycho Brahe had suggested that our satellite might be subject to forces exerted upon it by both the Sun and the Earth and varying with distance from these bodies. It therefore seemed important to secure information as to the relative distances of Sun and Moon from us such as eclipse observations could provide. As already related, Kepler had devised an instrument for determining how much of the solar disk was obscured by the Moon at an eclipse. He had employed this instrument on the eclipse of 1601, when the Moon was at its greatest distance from the Earth. At the forthcoming eclipse it would be at its nearest to the Earth; and a comparison of the two results should be useful.

Kepler successfully observed the impressive spectacle from the Imperial gardens, despite some interruption from the courtiers, whom the gardener was unable to keep at a convenient distance. He drew up a report on his observations; to this he appended an appeal to astronomers at large to tell him what they had seen of the phenomenon, and it was then printed and circulated throughout Europe by the Imperial ambassadors, the Jesuits and other agents with foreign connections. Kepler gleaned some useful information from the replies, particularly from material supplied by John Eriksen, sometime disciple of Tycho Brahe and now with Tengnagel at the London embassy, whose timing of the eclipse helped towards a more accurate estimation of the difference of longitude between Prague and London. Descriptions of the solar corona (the luminous outer envelope of the Sun) confirmed Kepler in the belief that space was filled with some aethereal substance illuminated by the eclipsed Sun.

CHAPTER TWELVE

THE NEW STAR OF 1604

In the autumn of 1604, as Kepler was summoning his ener-
gies for the final onslaught on the problem of Mars, his
attention was suddenly diverted by a startling and complicated celestial spectacle which challenged the expertise of
astrologers and filled the hearts of simple folk with fore-
boding. Basically, the phenomenon was a long-predicted one;
it was merely that the two planets, Jupiter and Saturn, appeared to approach close to each other in the sky through
happening to lie in nearly the same straight line as viewed
from the Earth. A third planet, Mars, was also (predictably) in
that part of the heavens about the same time, the three objects
forming an impressive group. But this so-called 'conjunction'
of Jupiter and Saturn occurred under circumstances of more
than ordinary interest to the astrologers, and its impressiveness
was enhanced beyond all expectation by the sudden appearance of a bright new star in the very midst of the planetary
concourse. The double event possessed a significance partly
fanciful, partly scientific.

Of merely fanciful interest was the conjunction of the two
planets. The ancient astronomers girdled the heavens with an
ideal circle or belt, marking the path which the seven 'planets'
were supposed to follow as they revolved round the central
Earth. This belt—the *zodiac*—was divided into twelve equal

arcs, or *signs*, of 30° each, reckoned from the point occupied by the Sun at the spring equinox. To each of these signs was attributed the nature of one of the four elements, fire, air, water and earth, taken in rotation, so that the first, fifth and ninth signs shared the nature of fire. Situated about the vertices of an equilateral triangle, these signs constituted what was called the 'fiery trigon', which was accorded pre-eminence over the trigons of the other elements since it contained the initial sign of the zodiac.

When, as happens from time to time, one planet overtakes another in its revolution round the heavens, the two are seen 'in conjunction' in the night sky; and these occasions were thought to be astrologically important. Now, as already stated, Jupiter completes a circuit round the heavens in about twelve years and Saturn in about thirty years; and a little reckoning with these figures will show that these two planets should be in conjunction once every twenty years, and that if one of these conjunctions falls in one sign of the 'fiery trigon', all the others should fall in the three fiery signs in turn. However, when more precise figures are used for the two planetary periods, it is found that the conjunctions work slowly round the zodiac, so that for two hundred years they fall in the fiery signs and, for the following six hundred years, outside of them; they are thus subject to a cycle of period eight hundred years.

Seven such cycles were reckoned to have occurred since the Creation; and now, at the beginning of the seventeenth century, an eighth cycle was about to commence with the expected appearance of Jupiter and Saturn conjoined in the fiery sign of the Archer. The onset of the previous cycles had been marked by the appearance on the Earth of Adam, Enoch, Noah . . . leading on to the Nativity and, lastly, the rise of Charlemagne. It was understandable, if irreverent, that Kepler should mark the forthcoming cycle with the name of his patron, the Emperor Rudolph. The inaugural conjunction was duly observed in December 1603, the presence of the planet Mars making the spectacle only more arresting.

It was in the company of these assembled planets that the marvellous new star appeared; and this star was, and remains, a matter of much greater scientific interest than the trivial conjunction of the planets in the sky. It is now well established that, from time to time, some barely noticeable star blows up or in some way enormously increases its brightness, so that in a few hours it comes to rival the most brilliant stars and planets in the heavens; it may even be visible in broad daylight. It then slowly fades, returning in a matter of months to its former insignificance. Passing over uncertain reports from earlier ages, the first historic outburst of this kind occurred in 1572 in the constellation Cassiopeia. Reference has already been made to this event; but it may now be explained, in a little more detail, how Tycho Brahe, Mästlin and other astronomers were able to prove beyond question that the object was situated in the celestial regions beyond the Moon; it was not, as was at first supposed, a mere explosion of vapours within the Earth's atmosphere.

One consequence of the daily rotation (whether of the Earth or of the heavens) must be that any object near the Earth exhibits, as it passes across the night sky, an apparent shift in relation to the background of stars. The nearer the object to us, the more pronounced is this so-called 'diurnal parallax'. The Moon appears to shift through a whole degree as it passes from the zenith to the horizon; it was clear, then, that the parallax of the new-born source of light, if atmospheric, should be even greater than that of the Moon and easily measurable. Now what Tycho Brahe and the other highly skilled observers established was that the mysterious object of 1572 exhibited *no* sensible diurnal parallax at all. It must therefore be situated in the depths of space far beyond the Moon and the planetary train: in short, it was a new *star*. This discovery that a spectacular change could occur in the supposedly unchangeable heavens helped to overthrow the traditional system of astronomy and to prepare the way for the scientific revolution of which Kepler was a pioneer. A fainter outburst of the same kind had occurred in the constellation of the Swan about 1600. And now another new star had blazed forth, this time in the constellation of Ophiucus the Serpent-holder, close to the venue of the planets in their 'great conjunction'.

Even to the modern historian the close coincidence of two such infrequent phenomena must seem remarkable. Its effect upon that astrologically minded generation was overwhelming. The Emperor Rudolph shared in full measure the superstitions of his subjects; and he set his Mathematician on observing and describing the new star with all diligence. Kepler welcomed the opportunity of discussing the scientific aspects, but he shrank from the tedious and perplexing task of spelling out the prophetic import, comparing himself to a beast of burden that could be compelled only by blows and curses to step into a puddle. He rushed into print with a German *Report* (1604); but his views on the phenomenon received a more considered and formal expression in his Latin treatise, *On the New Star in Serpentarius*, published in 1606, after he had got the theory of Mars off his hands and was free to reflect on this new cosmic conundrum. The book is typical of the occasional works, called forth by some celestial event or current controversy, that Kepler composed from time to time; it contrasts with his more systematic treatises. He had helped in the preparation of Tycho's last book, which set forth the Dane's mature conclusions on the new star of 1572; he was therefore well equipped to pass judgement on all the uncritical ideas to which this most recent apparition had given currency.

Kepler first heard about the new star from John Brunowski, a court official and keen amateur astronomer. On 9 October 1604 it was the turn of Jupiter and Mars to be in conjunction. On the day following, Brunowski, peering through a gap in the clouds to see how far the planets had moved apart, beheld *three* brilliant objects instead of the expected two. In great excitement he brought the news to Kepler who, however, remained incredulous until, on 17 October, a break in a spell of bad weather enabled him to see the group for himself. Several of the leading European astronomers, including Mästlin, had already sighted the *nova* (Kepler employs the term as we still do). Kepler went on observing the object as it slowly faded; he caught the last doubtful glimpse of it in 1606. Meanwhile he had been composing his book on the new star; we must now take a glance at its contents.

Like its predecessor of 1572, the star exhibited no diurnal parallax and must therefore be situated far beyond the limits of the solar system. Again, since it remained immobile from night to night, it could not be a comet; in fact, it appeared perfectly round, with no trace of a cometary tail. The nova twinkled with rainbow hues, a phenomenon that Kepler attributed to some intermittent contraction forcing out light as the contractions of the heart were supposed to drive the vital spirits through the body. Or perhaps the new star was a flame that had now gone out, having exhausted its fuel. The alternative possibility that it had faded from view by receding into the depths of a boundless space touched on the perilous doctrine of the infinity of the Universe, taught by the heretic Giordano Bruno, who had perished at the stake nearly seven years before. An infinite universe could have no recognizable centre; but Kepler always maintained that the solar system occupied a unique central position surrounded by a vast starless sphere of space. Outside of this lay a star-filled shell which, having an interior boundary, must have an exterior one also. The depth of this layer of stars was a matter for conjecture: the stars might be all equal in intrinsic brightness but at unequal distances from us, or all at the same distance but unequally bright in themselves. If, as Kepler surmised, the new star was composed of celestial material, that would explain why the recent series of novae (1572, 1600 and now 1604) had all blazed forth in the star-filled tract of the Milky Way, where one might expect such material to be particularly abundant. This matter might be fashioned into stars by some 'architectonic' faculty of nature such as was supposed to generate minerals and the lower forms of life on the Earth.

Following the scientific discussion of the nova of 1604 comes a short account, complete with its own title-page, of the star which flared up in 1600 in the constellation of the Swan. This tract is dedicated to Baron Hoffmann; he had lent Kepler the equipment necessary for determining the position of the object, Tycho's heirs having impounded the dead astronomer's instruments. There was some question whether the star, an object of the third magnitude, was really new; but Kepler, searching through the standard catalogues and through Tycho's observing registers, could find no reference to it. It is now known to be an irregular variable star having some of the properties of a nova; since 1715 it has been of the fifth magnitude. It did not show the characteristically steep decline in brightness; yet Kepler felt certain it was not a comet.

After this interlude Kepler returns reluctantly to unfolding the import of the new star: astrology he regarded as a 'disease', but the task of interpretation could not be evaded. Kepler's pronouncements on what the star presaged to mankind were intentionally vague and inconclusive. He could feel sure only that celestial influences, and not merely inanimate forces, governed the course of events here below, because the earthly is cognate with the heavenly. At the lowest level the weather was an indication of the Earth's response to these influences; plentiful harvests followed important planetary conjunctions, the wines of the Neckar being of particular excellence in those seasons. Signs in the heavens also affected men, partly through consciousness, as when some enterprise was undertaken in an auspicious hour, and partly through instinct, stirring up the general political unrest characteristic of that age. Men born under the new star would be revolutionaries. The return of the 'fiery trigon' could of itself produce no supernatural effects, such as the end of the world or the collapse of the Turks as a world-power, nor could it give rise to any developments more wonderful than had emerged during the previous century-and-a-half, in which the world, after a thousand years of sleep, seemed to have re-awakened. Kepler reviews the achievements of that period in law, trade, warfare, geographical discovery, mechanics, printing, freedom of discussion; he cites the liberation from Rome, the preaching of the Gospel overseas, the new theology, jurisprudence, medicine, astronomy: 'I think now at length the world is living, nay, going mad.' Little more could be dreamt of except the discovery of a new world or the invention of flying.

If supernatural effects of the new star were to be sought, it must be regarded as having appeared not by necessity or chance but by the counsel and foreknowledge of God. There was no significance in a merely *natural* event; neglect of this principle had led to various forms of divination, astrology among them, or to the worse impiety of reducing life to a routine regulated by celestial times and seasons. But God still speaks to us by signs. Why not openly? Perhaps so that man shall not be quite certain of the event until it happens. God speaks to us through the heavenly bodies, the work of His fingers, and through their harmonies, that we apprehend through geometry. And although Kepler adopted a sceptical attitude towards the elaborate system of prognostication that astrology had become, yet he believed that God, speaking in accommodated language to men, might address his admonitions to them through the celestial signs in which they believed. In any case the new star must have been kindled for our sakes, since from no other world would it have appeared alongside the conjoined planets (Kepler agreed with Tycho that other inhabited globes might well exist).

Kepler classifies portents into (1) those *against* nature, which relate to religion or its custodian, the Church (e.g. the signs given to Joshua and Hezekiah and the darkness at the Crucifixion); (2) those *beyond* nature, which relate to political revolutions (comets referring to kings and new stars to states), and (3) *natural but rare* events which relate to the common man and his necessities. The new star means the emergence of a new republic under which the world will find rest. Yet all such interpretations seemed too small for a prodigy such as the new star. Could it portend a general migration from Europe to America and the evangelization of the barbarians there? Or the collapse of Islam? Or the conversion of the Jews, that remarkable people as old as the world who live in idleness on our labours? Could it be the return of Christ in glory? But no: 'the Gospel must first be published among all nations.' However, the Emperor had not appointed Kepler to be a prophet but to carry on and complete the reformation of astronomy begun by Tycho Brahe.

There were two astrological writers whose views on the new star particularly attracted Kepler's criticisms. One of them was his fellow-countryman and friend since his Tübingen days, Helisaeus Röslin, a court physician of wide-ranging scientific interests. Extravagant in his prognostications, Röslin maintained a sceptical attitude towards the new astronomy, and he made an ideal sparring-partner for Kepler. He had predicted that the new star of 1572 and a comet that appeared in 1580 would exert their full influence as from the year 1604, when something surpassingly wonderful would occur. He hailed the nova of that year as the fulfilment of this prophecy and as marking the onset of a season of catastrophes for Christendom. It was this inference that Kepler vigorously denied; he held that, though signs in the heavens foreshadowed *something*, yet it was not given to men to say *what* before the event, unless by some divine illumination. Röslin replied in a tract on the *Fashions of the Present Time* (1609), explaining the delay in the predicted catastrophes and dealing with Kepler's criticisms. Kepler's counterblast, *A Reply to Röslin's Discourse* (1609), was composed in a few days and rapidly followed his rival's tract into print. It dealt point by point with the astrologer's objections and ranged over a wide field of cosmological topics—the Copernican theory, new stars and comets, the four elements, the planetary influences on human affairs. He concedes to Röslin a more than ordinary gift for foreseeing the future; but 'I would rather believe that God guided Röslin's thoughts in divining things to come than that He ran the world, including the human will, according to a cut-and-dried, uniform routine such as Röslin could predict by rule.'

Closely connected with the 'Reply to Röslin' was a tract by Kepler whose Latin title (*Tertius Interveniens*) might be loosely rendered 'A Third Man joins in the Fray'; or, as Edward Rosen renders it, 'Third Man in the Middle'. It was written in answer to another court physician, Philip Feselius, whose extreme opposition to all forms of astrology had proved as little to Kepler's taste as had Röslin's uncritical enthusiasm for the pseudo-science. The two protagonists were writing against each other; and Kepler took the liberty of joining in their 'private fight' in order to defend his own brand of 'natural' astrology, which he claimed to be based upon experience. Many favourite themes from earlier writings and anticipations of later developments appear in this vast round-up—the *species* flowing out from physically active bodies, the geometrically minded Earth-Soul receptive of the influences, not magic but psychic, of planets mutually situated in recognized 'aspects', the Moon's domination over moist things, swaying the tides and promoting the growth of herbs. Among prevalent beliefs here touched upon were those relating to 'signatures': the colours, forms and markings of plants were held to indicate their properties and medicinal uses.

CHAPTER THIRTEEN

COMETS AND SUNSPOTS

In 1607 there appeared, near the constellation of the Great Bear, a comet destined to become the most famous object of its kind in history. For this was one of three apparitions, occurring respectively in 1531, 1607 and 1682 (with a questionable earlier one in 1456), which Edmond Halley in 1705 linked together as representing successive returns of the same body to our skies. He assigned to it an elliptic orbit described in about seventy-five years; and when his prophecy of its next visitation, in 1758, was fulfilled, his hypothesis was generally accepted. Since then the object has made its expected returns in 1835 and 1910; and earlier recorded appearances have been traced back to pre-Christian times.

Already in 1577 Tycho Brahe and Michael Mästlin had applied to the bright comet of that year somewhat the same technique of observation as had served to establish the celestial location of the 'new star' of 1572, and they had reached a similarly disturbing conclusion: the comet's track lay far beyond the Moon. It came as no less of a shock to conservative astronomers that the comet was moving rapidly through the heavens apparently unimpeded by the crystalline spheres traditionally supposed to carry the planets round on their courses and without itself depending upon the operation of such a sphere.

It was on a September evening of 1607 that Kepler spotted

the comet of destiny as he stood on one of the bridges over the river Moldau in Prague, having just finished watching a firework display. He observed it throughout the month that it remained visible: and he published early in the following year a short tract written in German for popular reading. It gave currency to his view that, just as the ocean was supposed spontaneously to generate whales and sea-monsters, so the great spaces of the Universe everywhere produced comets. A comet was a condensation in the all-pervading aether, a celestial 'abscess' of impurities, partly transparent but capable of dimming the light of the Sun on certain important occasions. Space (so Kepler supposed) was as full of comets as the sea was of fish; but we could see only those that approached close enough to the Earth. The Sun's rays, passing through the comet, forced out some of its material to form the tail, pointing away from the Sun (there is some resemblance here to modern views), and ultimately destroyed the object completely. A comet was not self-luminous; the deflection of the tail might be attributed to refraction suffered by the Sun's rays in passing through the head of the comet or to the ejected matter being immediately brought to rest. Contact with a comet's tail could render the atmosphere impure and thereby cause widespread mortality; but it was through no direct causal connection, but rather through an underlying sympathy between Earth and heaven, that the formation of a new comet was accompanied by wars and disturbances of the natural order here below. Kepler felt compelled to take some account of these astrological implications that so obsessed his contemporaries and were giving rise to a flood of prognostications. He thought that a comet, steered perhaps by astrologically minded daemons, might be sent by God as a sign (like a sea-monster washed ashore) to be understood by superstitious men in the sense He intended. However, the astronomer did venture one or two predictions on his own account.

Kepler promised that his little German tract would soon be followed by a Latin edition firmly establishing his views on the place and motion of comets. But publication was hindered by various circumstances. The theologians objected to the idea of cometary daemons newly created; the printer caused a delay and then said that people had lost interest in the comet; noblemen to whom the various parts of the book had been dedicated kept dying and fresh ones had to be found. In 1618 three comets appeared within a few months of one another, as if to mark the outbreak of the Thirty Years' War; and this afforded Kepler an excuse for bringing out his *Three Tracts on Comets* at Augsburg in the following year.

Like the German dissertation, the book falls into three parts, astronomical, physical, astrological. It takes up the problem, posed by Tycho and Mästlin, of determining the distance and motion of a comet. However, as a Copernican, Kepler had to reckon with the parallax exhibited by the object in consequence of the Earth's annual revolution; this was both a complication to be allowed for and an aid to locating the planet in space. The geometry of cometary parallax is set forth in thirty propositions and then applied to all available observations of the four visitants under review; but the problem was really indeterminate for Kepler, and his scanty data could be fitted to almost any preconceived orbit. He nowhere attempts a physical explanation of cometary motion such as he had of planetary. Aristotelian ideas had still weighed sufficiently with Tycho Brahe and Mästlin for them to assign to the comet of 1577 (as to a *celestial* body) a circular orbit close to that of Venus. But Kepler, reflecting the same tradition with a difference, felt that a circular or elliptic orbit, appropriate to an enduring and divinely appointed planet, did not befit a body as transient as a comet. It also seemed unreasonable to assign a closed orbit to a body that was never seen to return to its starting-point in the heavens. So he preferred the view that comets travelled in straight lines with regularly varying speeds.

Kepler's views on the 'natural history' of comets had undergone but little development since he put them on paper in Prague twelve years before, though they differed in some respects from the ideas he entertained when he wrote his 'Supplement to Witelo' of 1604. Of the three comets of 1618, Kepler surmised that the second and third were portions of a single object that had broken in two (as Biela's comet was to do in 1845). As for the astrology of comets, Kepler claimed that some of his predictions from the visitation of 1607 had been fulfilled, others had not. However, a comet's significance is not to be interpreted according to fixed rules; the sign is 'angled' at those for whom it is intended, as the serenade is addressed to the ear of the beloved.

The three comets of 1618, affording an occasion for the publication of Kepler's cometary treatise, served also as a signal for rekindling the controversy as to the place of such objects in the scheme of things. In his *Anti-Tycho* of 1621, the Italian astronomer Scipione Chiaramonti launched a strong but reasoned attack upon the cometary theories of Tycho Brahe, now twenty years dead. When, at last, in 1624, Kepler obtained a copy of the book from the Jesuit mathematician Paul Guldin, his good friend at court, he felt called upon to defend his old master against the Italian's attack. With natural piety there may have mingled a desire to improve his relations with Tycho's heirs and so to remove obstacles to his hoped-for publication of the *Rudolphine Tables*. Or he may have yielded to pressure from Guldin: the Jesuits were on Tycho's side in the matter of comets, as we shall see in a moment.

Whatever the motives, Kepler published his *Hyperaspistes*—the 'Champion' (of Tycho Brahe)—in 1625. He must have begrudged the time spent on this his last polemic writing; it is ungracious in tone and it contains nothing new of scientific interest. Chiaramonti replied at length, but Kepler made no further rejoinder. When the book was in the press, however, he hastily added an appendix reflecting yet another episode in the controversy over comets.

Inspired by the same cometary spectacle of 1618, a Jesuit mathematician, Horatio Grassi, delivered a public lecture on comets at the Collegio Romano, in the course of which he upheld Tycho Brahe's thesis that these objects can occur in a region of space more remote than the Moon; he further maintained that their orbits must be circular. Galileo, mistaken for once in a scientific judgement, held that comets were indeed atmospheric condensations and that what we see of them was an optical phenomenon comparable to mock-suns or haloes. In any case, he thought their extravagant orbits could not be those of heavenly bodies. Those were difficult years for Galileo, and he preferred that his attempt to refute Grassi should appear under the name of his disciple Mario Guiducci. Grassi countered by replying under the name 'Sarsio'; Galileo struck back in his turn in 1623 with his 'Assayer' (*Il Saggiatore*), one of his most brilliant controversial pieces. When Paul Guldin brought Chiaramonti's book to Kepler, he had with him also a copy of the 'Assayer'; but, being on a hurried journey, he could permit the astronomer only a fleeting glimpse of Galileo's little volume. Later, Kepler obtained a copy of the 'Assayer' from Guldin; and he replied to all the supposed reflections on Tycho Brahe in an appendix to his *Hyperaspistes*. The episode had the unfortunate effect of widening the rift between Kepler and Galileo.

In a postscript to his German tract on the comet of 1607,

Kepler referred to another celestial phenomenon that he had observed in this same year and of which he published a fuller account two years later. An examination of planetary tables had convinced him that, on 29 May 1607, the planet Mercury would pass directly between the Earth and the Sun. He thought that, in this situation, the planet might be visible for a short time as a dark spot silhouetted against the solar disk. When a severe storm occurred on the 27th, he feared that the conjunction had taken place earlier than he expected, upsetting the weather. However, on the 28th, allowing the Sun's rays to pass through a small hole into a darkened room, he formed the solar image upon a screen; and there, some way from the centre, was a dark spot which he likened to a small fly or flea and took to be the planet in process of transit. Kepler fled to the palace to inform the Emperor; he repeated the observation in various places, and he secured independent witnesses to countersign his written narrative.

Already in his 'Supplement to Witelo', Kepler had cited a Frankish chronicler of the age of Charlemagne who had reported the observation of what was believed to be a transit of Mercury occurring about the year A.D. 807. Mästlin believed the story to relate to a prodigy: the details were contradictory, and he thought that Mercury was transparent and therefore invisible in transit. Kepler's account of the supposed transit is in two parts: first, a critical restoration and analysis of the chronicler's text, and then the narrative of his own observations. Some concluding verses blend the joy of discovery with sorrow for the death of the little daughter of his patron Wackher von Wackenfels.

After all this, it must have been a disappointment to Kepler to realize that he had been completely mistaken, like the Frankish annalist before him. There can be no doubt that what he saw was a large sunspot. Had he repeated his observation on the succeeding days, he would have noticed that the phenomenon persisted beyond the possible duration of a transit of Mercury; and he would have enjoyed priority over the observers—Johann Fabricius, Scheiner, Galileo—who, a few years later, were to establish the existence of sunspots with the aid of the telescope. Following the discovery of the spots, Kepler admitted his error. There was the consolation that a close study of the sunspots established the axial rotation of the Sun that Kepler had already assumed as an hypothesis necessary to explain the orbital revolution of the planets. Yet, against Mästlin and other authorities, Kepler still maintained that it should be possible to observe Mercury in transit. In 1629 he predicted such a phenomenon for 1631, when it was indeed observed for the first time by the French scientist Pierre Gassend; but Kepler did not live to see it.

CHAPTER FOURTEEN

THE TRIUMPHS OF THE
TELESCOPE

A new chapter in the history of astronomy opened early in the seventeenth century with the establishment of the practice of combining a concave with a convex lens to produce magnified images of distant and eventually of celestial objects. To pass over isolated claims from earlier ages to the discovery of some such device, this primitive form of the telescope seems to have been effectively invented in Holland, probably at Middelburg, about 1608. News of the invention, and examples of the instrument itself, spread rapidly through western and southern Europe. The reports reached the ears of Galileo Galilei, then a Professor at Padua. Working on hints and utilizing the known refractive properties of glass, he was able to construct an instrument that already took the familiar form of a tube with a lens at each end.

Galileo, indeed, developed no physical theory of the mode of operation of the telescope; but he established once for all the practice of examining heavenly bodies through such instruments. True, his achievements in this field seem to have been closely paralleled in England by another of Kepler's occasional correspondents, Thomas Harriot. And for all the attention they have received from historians, Galileo's telescopic discoveries can be regarded as representing only an isolated episode in a career devoted predominantly to the reformation of mechanics. He described his earliest celestial observations in a little book, 'The Starry Messenger', or, perhaps better, 'The Starry Message' (*Sidereus Nuncius*), published in March 1610. The book was chiefly notable for its announcement of Galileo's discovery of the four principal satellites of the planet Jupiter. The news quickly reached the ears of other European astronomers. To none can it have struck home with such shattering force as to Kepler.

The *New Astronomy* had lately appeared and Kepler was relaxing after the final effort of publishing it; but his mind kept running on Galileo, wondering whether he would break his twelve years' silence with some words of commendation for the new book. It was at such a moment that Kepler's friend Wackher von Wackenfels stopped his carriage outside the astronomer's house and, without descending, called out to him that Galileo had discovered four new planets. Kepler wondered how such a thing could be, the scheme of his *Cosmographic Mystery* making provision only for the six planets already known. Perhaps Galileo had discovered four little moons, one apiece for the planets Saturn, Jupiter, Mars and Venus; if Mercury, too, possessed such a companion the glare of the Sun would make it difficult to descry. Wackher thought the new planets might be revolving round fixed stars; but that savoured of the 'horrid philosophy' of the heretic Giordano Bruno, who had maintained that the stars were suns, each with its train of inhabited planets. Further surmise was ended by the arrival of Galileo's 'Starry Messenger' in Prague.

Since his brief correspondence with Galileo concerning the *Cosmographic Mystery*, Kepler had published his 'Supplement to Witelo' and his *New Astronomy*; but Galileo had remained unaware of the former and he showed no appreciation of the great importance of the latter. Hence it must have been with some surprise that, on 8 April 1610, Kepler received through the Tuscan Ambassador a copy of the 'Messenger' and (on the 13th) an invitation from Galileo himself to appraise its claims. He had, indeed, already been allowed to skim through a copy by the Emperor, who also wanted to know his opinion of the work. Rudolph, too, had looked at the Moon through a glass earlier the same year, and he had fancied that the Earth's continents and seas could be seen mirrored in the lunar surface. This would seem the appropriate place to say a word about the contents of the historic book thus placed in Kepler's hands, and in which its illustrious author first openly signified his assent to the Copernican planetary theory. We can then go on to look at Kepler's comments on its contents.

Directing his telescope (it magnified lengths upwards of thirtyfold) first towards the Moon, Galileo beheld, not the perfect polished sphere of classical tradition, but an uneven globe, its surface diversified with mountains and valleys like those familiar to us on the Earth. Here was another stage in the process of breaking down the artificial distinction between the Earth and the heavenly bodies. That these irregularities did not appear in silhouette against the sky at the limb (or edge) of the Moon, giving the appearance of a toothed wheel, was (so Galileo maintained) because our view through gaps between the mountains was interrupted by more distant elevations. Or perhaps the Moon possessed a dense atmosphere reflecting the sunlight and presenting its greatest thickness obliquely to our view at the Moon's limb so as to cloak the lunar periphery. Perhaps this was why the illuminated portion of the Moon seemed to have a bigger radius than the shaded part. Galileo established a classic procedure for estimating the height of a lunar mountain by finding its distance from the line dividing light and dark on the Moon at the instant when the peak began to be illuminated. He also explained why, particularly around new moon, the shadowed portion of the lunar disk sometimes shines with a dim light, giving the phenomenon known as 'the old moon in the arms of the new'. It is caused by 'earthshine', sunlight reflected from the Earth and falling on the Moon.

When Galileo turned his telescope to the stars, he noticed that they were not magnified in anything like the same proportion as the Moon. He referred this to the illusion that makes the unaided eye over-estimate the size of an intensely luminous object owing to what we call 'irradiation'. The telescope deprived the stars of their adventitious aureoles and merely magnified (or so Galileo supposed) their 'simple globes' (in actual fact, no star exhibits a perceptible true disk even in the most powerful telescope). Galileo's instrument vastly increased the number of stars visible; and it appeared to resolve the Milky Way and certain nebulous patches on the night sky into aggregations of stars. Galileo further explained how the telescope could be used for measuring the angular separation of a pair of stars close together on the vault of the sky; he thus anticipated a very important application of the instrument not to be seriously utilized, however, until about fifty years later.

Most of the discoveries so far mentioned had been anticipated in some degree by earlier writers; but Galileo was the first to *see* these things. However, the 'Messenger' goes on to announce Galileo's unheralded discovery, early in January 1610, of four 'planets' (it was Kepler who introduced the term 'satellite') revolving round Jupiter and accompanying that planet in its course through the zodiacal constellations. He even noticed the fluctuations in the brightness of these objects. Galileo named the four satellites the 'Medicean stars' in honour of his patron Cosimo II de' Medici, the Grand Duke of Tuscany. Galileo emphasized how the existence of Jupiter's moons (the 'Circum-Jovialists', as English astronomers later termed them) exploded the anti-Copernican argument that our Moon, revolving round the Earth, could not at the same time accompany the Earth in an annual revolution round the Sun.

Galileo's discoveries did not accord with the orthodox natural philosophy of his day. The optical working of the telescope had not been explained, so that it was not unreasonable to regard things seen through it as visual 'ghosts'. In any case, many of Galileo's colleagues, through inexperience and the deficiencies of the instrument, were honestly unable to see the Jovian moons. There was, besides, much personal hostility to Galileo on various grounds; this found expression in such publications as Martin Horky's *Pilgrimage against the Starry Messenger* (1610). In this situation, Galileo was glad to seek support from Kepler, the Imperial Mathematician, despite the long silence between them.

For his part, Kepler was at the disadvantage of never having seen a telescope, let alone the marvels alleged to have been descried with its aid. It was impossible for his response to be merely factual, as the 'Messenger' had claimed to be; and as an astronomer he was bound to be drawn into the cosmological conflict which Galileo had largely avoided. He kept hoping he would receive a telescope from Galileo, who was handing them out to potentates. He even tried to make one for himself, using the indifferent lenses available at Prague. He was already thinking out the optical rationale of the instrument and was suggesting improvements, such as the use of lenses of hyperbolic section. But the glass obtainable at Prague was not of optical quality, and the lens grinders were not co-operative.

However, Kepler took a chance and agreed to write a *Conversation with the Starry Messenger*, in the form of a letter to

Galileo but suitable for publication; and he finished it by 19 April, in time for the same courier as had brought the book to take it back with him to Tuscany. It was printed in an enlarged version by the middle of May 1610.[1] By calling his book a 'conversation', Kepler implied that Galileo had intended his title to bear the meaning of 'Messenger'; and Galileo's enemies accordingly accused him of calling *himself* a 'heavenly messenger'!

Kepler followed the arguments of Galileo's book point by point. He suggested that the shadowed depressions seen on the Moon might be walled areas designed to protect the inhabitants from the fierce heat of the Sun; or they might be pores in a lunar crust of pumice. Was Galileo sure that the edge of the Moon appeared perfectly regular? That was not Kepler's impression. He claimed the explanation of 'earthshine' for his master, Mästlin; in fact, it goes back to Leonardo da Vinci. Turning to the section on the stars, Kepler gives a physiological explanation of why they appear larger to the eye than the telescope reveals them to be: in the darkness the pupil of the eye is dilated and a sharp retinal image is no longer formed. It was characteristic of Kepler's preoccupation with the quantitative aspects of phenomena that he attached particular importance to Galileo's plan for measuring small celestial angles. Maintaining the uniqueness of the solar system, and with some anticipation of what came to be known as 'Olbers's Paradox', Kepler argues that, if a thousand stars were massed together in the sky, their aggregate size would appear about equal to that of the Sun. If all the stars were put together they would exceed the Sun in apparent size. Why, then, if the stars are suns, do they not give us more light than

[1] See E. Rosen, *Kepler's Conversation with Galileo's Sidereal Messenger, First complete Translation, with an Introduction and Notes,* New York and London, 1965.

119

the Sun? Are they too far away? But the farther they are, the bigger they must be. It cannot be that the aether obscures them, for we see their disks and scintillations. From the weakness of starlight Kepler infers that the Sun is vastly more luminous than any star, and our system is not merely one of a herd. Again, if there are other systems, they must be either exactly like ours or different. If alike, there must be a Galileo observing in each of them; but what would be the good of such endless repetition? If they are different, they must be built up round schemes other than that of the five regular solids and thus be less noble than our system. Hence ours has the pre-eminence over any others.

As for the Jovian moons, they keep so close to their planet that no separate account need be taken of them by astrologers. To explain their reported variations in brightness, Kepler makes the interesting suggestion (anticipating the modern view of this phenomenon) that the satellites are non-spherical and do not turn the same faces to us in all situations. Perhaps the moons were assigned to the Jovians to compensate them for not being able to descry Mercury or other remote planets. Kepler looked forward, if only in fantasy, to the day when human settlers, having discovered the art of flying, would colonize the Moon and the planet Jupiter; after all, it was safer to cross the ocean than the English Channel. Meanwhile, man was never meant to remain in the centre of the Universe but to go voyaging round on his ship, the Earth.

For a time Kepler feared he had been premature in his championship of Galileo, especially when he learned that a demonstration of the telescope and its powers, arranged for the Bologna professors, had ended in fiasco. From this uncertainty he was delivered, in the summer of 1610, by the loan, for about ten days, of a Galilean telescope brought from Vienna by the Elector Ernst of Cologne; he had come to

Prague to attend a conference of princes called to settle differences between the Emperor and his brother Matthias. Gazing
through the instrument, Kepler observed such of the satellites
of Jupiter as he could distinguish from night to night. He
shared the telescope with friends who made independent
drawings of what they saw for subsequent comparison; and
he published the results in his *Narration concerning the four
satellites of Jupiter* (1610), to be checked against any observations meanwhile recorded by Galileo, with whom he had no
communications at that period. About this time Galileo published his anagram relating to the anomalous appearance of
the planet Saturn; Kepler rearranged the letters into a sen-
tence suggesting satellites for Mars, and he spent some time
searching vainly for such attendants upon the ruddy planet.

The mysterious capabilities of the telescope directed Kepler's attention once again to the science of light. His treatise of
1604 had seemed to contain everything that could usefully be
said about the subject. But now he returned to it to compose
what has come to be regarded as the earliest recognizable
textbook of geometrical optics as we understand the term
today. Kepler called his book the 'Dioptrics' (*Dioptrice*), coin-
ing the word to express the idea of light *passing through* a
transparent medium, on the analogy of the Greek word
Catoptrice, relating to rays *incident upon* a reflecting surface. In
the foreword he was able to publish Galileo's announcement
(now unriddled) of the discovery of the appendages of Saturn
and of the Moon-like phases of Venus.

The 'Dioptrics', while re-presenting some of the earlier
material for the sake of completeness, is written in a more
impersonal style; it breaks free from the medieval mould of
the former treatise, attaining greater lucidity and a more
mathematical and diagrammatic treatment. Still without an
exact law of refraction, Kepler assumed, as was sufficiently

near the truth for his purpose, that, for angles of incidence less than 30°, the angle of refraction was proportional to the angle of incidence, the ratio (for refraction from air to glass) being as 2 to 3. His experiment for determining this ratio is shown in Figure 9. Rays of sunlight L, M, N, passing the edge

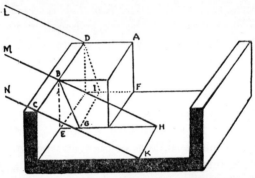

9. Kepler's Method of Determining the Refraction of Light by Glass

CD, go partly through the glass cube BDAF and partly to the side of it, forming on the graduated base of the instrument two shadows, IG and HK, from the lengths of which the required angles can be deduced.

Kepler proceeded to trace graphically the course of light rays through various types of lenses or lens combinations, the optical properties of which he was thus the first to elucidate. He limited his consideration to rays departing but little from the axes of these systems and thus subject to his approximate law of refraction. Of particular interest is the case where a convex and a concave lens are employed in conjunction, as in Galileo's form of the telescope. Kepler also investigated the optical properties of two convex lenses, conjoined to give a magnified, inverted image of a distant object, thus anticipating the form of the telescope that has established itself for astronomical purposes. However, he did not venture to identify this combination as a *telescope*, and he lacked the means for its practical construction. The earliest 'Keplerian', or astronomical, telescope seems to have been fashioned some twenty years later by Christopher Scheiner, who also put into practice Kepler's design for a combination of *three* convex lenses to give an upright image.

The 'Dioptrics' also presents Kepler's more considered views on the physiology of vision. 'Sight is the sensation of an affection of the retina.' When the lens of the eye forms its retinal image of the distant scene, a change is produced in the 'visual spirit' (*spiritus visivus*) permeating the retina; this is proved (as Alhazen had already argued) by the persistence of after-images when the eyes are closed. However, the formation of the retinal image does not constitute the entire act of seeing; something has to be transmitted to the seat of the faculty of sight in the brain. This transmission might be effected by the optic nerves, whose chief function (so Kepler supposed) was to convey visual spirit to the eyes. Perhaps the retinal impression travelled up the spirit-filled nerves (as a disturbance travels outward when a stone is dropped into a pool) until it reached the brain, where *something* reconstructs the image. Kepler grappled with what he felt to be the problems of why, when the retinal image is inverted, we see things the right way up, and why, having two eyes, we see but one image. He thought the ciliary processes, which in fact control the curvature of the lens, served to alter the shape of the eyeball and hence the distance between lens and retina; and he compared this adjustment to the automatic enlargement or contraction of the pupil in response to changes in the intensity of the light entering the eye.

Kepler wrote his 'Dioptrics' in haste as he expected to have to leave Prague at any time. He handed the manuscript to the Elector Ernst of Cologne, to whom he had dedicated the work and through whose good offices it was published at Augsburg in 1611. Kepler was too much overwhelmed by personal misfortunes to send out the customary presentation copies to the leading men of science of his day, and the 'Dioptrics' aroused little immediate interest. But, on a longer view, its influence on the progress of optics was decisive, particularly in England, where two further editions of the treatise appeared in the course of the seventeenth century.

CHAPTER FIFTEEN

FROM PRAGUE TO LINZ

The completion and publication of the *New Astronomy* marked the onset of an increasingly acute political crisis in Bohemia, destined eventually to end Kepler's close association with the Emperor Rudolph and to send him forth on yet another stage of his life's pilgrimage. The Emperor's eccentricities had grown upon him, and his empire was passing under the control of his brother, the Archduke Matthias. At the moment, developments favoured the Protestants; but Kepler found the long-term prospects disquieting. In 1609 he had journeyed to Heidelberg to supervise the printing of his book, and he had visited the Frankfurt book fair. On the way home he passed through Swabia and called on his friends at Tübingen. He was anxious to explore the possibilities of returning there in some capacity. At the same time he addressed himself to the Duke of Württemberg, ostensibly craving permission to seek another appointment abroad, but, in fact, with the possibility in mind of entering the Duke's service. In order to avoid future complications should the Duke recall him, Kepler frankly confessed the intellectual difficulties he felt over the strict Lutheran doctrine of 'ubiquity', particularly as it had come to be embodied in what was called the Formula of Concord. According to this article of belief, Christ is present in body as well as in spirit, not only in the sacramental elements but *everywhere*. Against this view (which the Calvinists rejected and which the Lutherans did not long retain) Kepler appealed to what he regarded as a more authoritative tradition based upon the Scriptures and the Fathers. He was granted the freedom of movement he sought; the religious issues he raised were not taken up for the moment.

The year 1611 proved one of the most tragic in the annals of Kepler's chequered life-story, and it marked the break-up of his career at Prague. Yet he began the year cheerfully enough with the dispatch of a seasonable offering (*Strena*) to his patron and fellow-countryman Wackher von Wackenfels. It took the form of a disquisition, half playful, half scientific, on the geometry of snow crystals. These gems of winter's fashioning exhibit a basically hexagonal structure; and Kepler could not conceive this to be a matter of chance. Nor could he suppose that the formless, invisible vapour, raised from the ground by heat, should without more ado condense itself into such an ornate configuration. Some formative agent must be at work, whether acting from without or innate in the material as an archetype of the beauty of the hexagonal form, or as foreseeing some end to which that form would conduce. The phenomenon brought to Kepler's mind the hexagonal form of the cells of a honeycomb, which completely fill up the space they jointly occupy with a minimum expenditure of wax. They form a double layer, the internal apex of each cell lying in the depression between three adjacent cells on the opposite side, so that each larva has nine neighbours; the geometrical relations involved recalled some of the properties of the regular solids. Comparison was suggested also with the arrangement of grains in a pomegranate and the symmetrical grouping of the petals and other components of a flower, often in fives or tens. Returning to the original problem,

Kepler likens snow crystals to chemical salts; and he approaches later theories of crystal structure with his discussion of the several ways in which spheres can be packed together in space. However, unsupported by anything in the way of an atomic theory of matter, his reflections led to no satisfying conclusion.

As the tragic year 1611 drew on, Kepler's home circle was shattered by the deaths, first, of his promising six-year-old son, Frederick, and then, in July, of his wife Barbara. Meanwhile, civil war had reached Prague. The Emperor Rudolph had completely lost his grasp of the political situation. His cousin Leopold, Bishop of Passau, bringing up an army supposedly in support of Rudolph, had occupied part of Prague against local resistance; and when these forces had been bought off, the Archduke Matthias was left in control. Rudolph was compelled to abdicate and Matthias became King of Bohemia and, in due course, Emperor. Efforts were made from several quarters to involve Kepler in the struggle in his capacity of an astrologer able to discern which of the contending parties might expect to be favoured by the celestial influences. While scrupulous to avoid giving comfort to his master's enemies, Kepler was equally careful not to encourage the Emperor in any imprudent venture.

One consequence of these political upheavals was that Kepler's official position became increasingly precarious; and the downfall of his Imperial patron gave a new urgency to the plans that had long been forming in his mind for leaving Prague. He turned again to his homeland and the ducal house of Württemberg; and steps were taken to secure for him the Chair of Mathematics at Tübingen in succession to his former teacher, Mästlin, now grown old (yet destined to outlive the astronomer). However, the theological authorities there vetoed Kepler's appointment on the ground of his admitted

leanings towards Calvinism. There was talk of his going to
Padua to succeed Galileo; but in the end he accepted an
appointment as District Mathematician at Linz, the capital of
Upper Austria, with the duties of teaching school and map-
ping the locality. Kepler had hoped that his wife would be
happier there than she had been at Prague, which lay so much
farther from Graz. But before the move could be made,
Barbara Kepler had died of typhus, spread through the
Bohemian capital by the invading soldiery. She left no will;
and the division of her possessions among her children was
accompanied by the usual contention and litigation in which
it seemed to be Kepler's fate always to be involved. Rudolph,
though now deposed, was still alive; and at his entreaty
Kepler put off his migration to remain with the ex-Emperor
until he died early in 1612. Then Kepler was free to depart;
and he arrived at Linz in May of that year. The new Emperor
Matthias confirmed Kepler in the office and emoluments of
Imperial Mathematician; but he did not share the scientific
interests of his predecessor or require that the astronomer
should reside at court. It sufficed that he should be somewhere
within reach; and this confirmed Kepler in his choice of an
abode at Linz, which the Emperor expressly approved.

After the social and intellectual life of Prague, Kepler must
have found Linz something of a backwater. At the Imperial
court, his stimulating if sometimes inharmonious dialogue
with Tycho Brahe on planetary theory had broadened with
the passing years into debate on more fundamental issues with
other aristocratic scholars whose friendship he enjoyed. As
the Emperor's confidant, he found himself at the centre of the
political web. But Linz was a mere provincial capital; and
Kepler's very superiority to local levels and standards in
matters of the mind and spirit attracted adverse notice and
awakened resentment. Once again, as in Graz, he found him-

self a mere assistant master, subordinated to the petty tyrant of a district school.

At Linz, too, Kepler was immediately subjected to vexatious persecution such as he had not experienced in the freer spiritual atmosphere of Prague. The pressure came not from the Catholic party, which was in a minority in Upper Austria, but from the authorities of Kepler's own Lutheran denomination, who followed the strict line laid down in Württemberg and defined in the Formula of Concord. Kepler declined to sign this document without reservations as to its doctrine of the Sacrament; and he was forthwith excluded from communion and thereby expelled from the congregation. The astronomer appealed to the Stuttgart consistory, the board of clergy appointed to supervise Church affairs, who in fact controlled the congregation at Linz; but his plea was elaborately rejected. Meanwhile, his teaching activities were hampered, and an attempt was made to terminate his employment in the interests of economy.

Nevertheless, Kepler remained at Linz for fourteen years, his longest stay at any one place. He found some compensation for the disagreeable circumstances of his position in the society and stimulating converse of a group of scholarly noblemen, who had secured his appointment and, indeed, caused a vacancy to be created for him. He resolved not to move until he should have prepared the great set of planetary tables that it had so long been his intention to publish as it had been Tycho Brahe's before him, and which were now to be completed under the patronage of the house of Austria.

Within eighteen months of his settlement at Linz, Kepler married again. Following the death of his first wife, his affections were for a time unsettled, and various possibilities were weighed; but eventually his choice fell upon Susanna Reuttinger, an orphan of humble birth, seventeen years younger than the bridegroom. He met her in the household of a noble-man whose wife had cared for her from childhood. They were married in October 1613, and the Emperor Matthias was present at the wedding, thereby helping to dispel the impression that Kepler was marrying beneath him. A happy home life now began for the astronomer, such as he had never known before and in which his two motherless children fully shared. By his second wife he had six more children, of whom, however, only the three youngest survived infancy. Kepler was a devoted father, zealous in the education and religious instruction of his children. He prepared German versions of Latin texts for the use of his son Louis, and he composed a catechism on the Sacrament for the children to commit to memory.

CHAPTER SIXTEEN

MEASURING TIME AND WINE

During his early years at Linz, Kepler published several books which, though not of any great consequence to science, yet serve to show his mathematical expertise operating in unfamiliar settings. On the one hand, the Imperial mathematician applied himself to problems of chronology, the art of dating historic events. And, in contrast, in the role of a prudent householder, he found himself called upon to gauge the contents of wine-casks.

Kepler lived in an age greatly exercised about questions of chronology, an art lately established through the labours of Joseph Scaliger. For the first time it had become possible to make a sober comparison of the record of Scripture with the annals and monuments of general history; and it was with an understandable sense of urgency that efforts were made to remove discrepancies between sacred and profane chronology. The reckoning of time was involved also in the controversy that broke out over the reformed calendar introduced by Pope Gregory XIII in 1582, when Kepler would be ten years old. The astronomer wrote in favour of the Gregorian calendar; but unfortunately it had been introduced too late to be accepted unanimously by an undivided Christendom, hence the confessional conflict that it excited. It was not adopted in Protestant Germany until 1700, when the astronomer had been in his grave for seventy years.

Chronology possessed a strange fascination for Kepler, as it did for Isaac Newton. Initiated into its subtleties by his teacher Michael Mästlin and later plied with questions on Roman history by the Bavarian Chancellor, Herwart von Hohenburg, he came to find in chronological exercises a source of relaxation and refreshment in seasons of depression or overstrain, such as the ominous months that preceded his forced departure from Prague. Much of Kepler's work on chronology remained unprinted or unfinished or has disappeared altogether. The half-dozen works that he published in this field all dealt with biblical chronology, and chiefly with dating the Nativity, Ministry and Passion of our Lord.

In the summer of 1605 Kepler spent a few weeks in Styria attending to personal concerns. While at Graz he bought a little book by a Pole, Laurentius Suslyga, on the historical problem of dating the birth of Christ. It had already been suggested that the Nativity did not coincide precisely with the beginning of the Christian Era but fell several years earlier. Suslyga thought the discrepancy might be as much as four years. Kepler, who had already discussed the problem, was taken with the book and decided to append a summary of its contents to his forthcoming treatise on the New Star. However, he differed from Suslyga about the vital date of a lunar eclipse that occurred shortly before the death of Herod the Great. This put the Nativity back another year and made the probable date of the appearance of the Star of Bethlehem coincide with that of a threefold conjunction of planets just preceding the onset of the sixth series (since the Creation) of great planetary conjunctions falling in the 'fiery trigon'. Thus the Star of Bethlehem could be regarded as in some sense the counterpart of the nova of 1604. Kepler confessed himself to have strayed into a 'chronological thicket'; and the printer, on his own responsibility, gave this title (*Sylva Chronologica*) to the little tract.

Kepler developed his views on the problem of dating the Nativity in controversial tracts and letters, both Latin and German, addressed particularly to his old opponent Röslin and to one Seth Kallwitz (Calvisius), a Church musician who made a hobby of chronology. He attacked the considerations on which Dionysius Exiguus had fixed the epoch, or starting-point, of the Christian Era. That obscure sixth-century chronologist had relied upon extra-biblical traditions in dating the conception of St. John the Baptist and consequentially the birth of Christ. Kepler approaches the problem through the Gospel story, the narrative of Josephus, the stock-in-trade of the classical scholar, and, less acceptably to our way of thinking, the astronomy and astrology of the spectacular planetary conjunction which he deemed to have set the Wise Men upon their quest. Kepler believed the Star of Bethlehem to have been *supernatural*, which was the view he had taken of the 'new star' of 1604. Yet the three Wise Men would seem to have thought that they knew the significance of the Star as if it were part of the *natural* order covered by the rules of astrology. Could it not have been the conjunction of Jupiter, Saturn and Mars occurring in the year 6 B.C. that, in fact, attracted the notice of the Wise Men? When Kepler came round to that view he tried to date the Nativity by reference to the conjunction and laid correspondingly less stress upon the Star. Turning from astrology to purely historical considerations, and taking at their face value all the recorded circumstances—the birth of the Baptist, the taxing under Cyrenius, the coming of the Magi, the slaughter of the Innocents, the death of Herod the Great—he finds himself confirmed in the view, still broadly held today, that the Nativity must be placed a full five years before the epoch marking the conventional inception of the Christian era.

Turning now to a very different theme, we have to relate

how a simple problem of domestic arithmetic started Kepler upon his most ambitious excursion into the realm of pure geometry. The ancient civilizations carried their arts of reckoning to various levels of refinement; but there was nothing to compare to the Greek discipline of propositional geometry, familiar to us today through textbooks deriving from Euclid. The Babylonians and Egyptians, the Indians and Chinese possessed prescriptions for estimating the areas of rectilinear figures, both plane and solid; but the Greeks succeeded in establishing the mensuration of the circle and its derivatives, and even of certain conic segments, by proofs of the utmost rigour. Mathematicians of Kepler's day were willing to sacrifice some of this rigour for the sake of shorter proofs; they were trying to formulate a standard procedure, such as the calculus was later to afford, for handling continuously varying quantities and the curves that serve to represent these. Kepler was deeply versed in Greek mathematics and ingenious in performing what were essentially integrations, as required for the construction of his planetary theories, but he had never shown much taste for geometry in the abstract, being more interested in results than in proofs.

In 1613 the Austrian vineyards yielded an abundance of excellent wine. Barges carried the overplus to all the Danubian lands, and the wharves of Linz were piled high with casks of the generous liquor, on sale at reasonable prices. Kepler, starting married life, deemed it wise to stock his cellar. He laid in several barrels; and a few days later the vintner called to estimate their capacity and to make out his bill. It was the custom to determine the volume of a cask by inserting a gauging-rod through the bung-hole, finding how far it would go, and then reading the capacity off the graduated rod without regard to the shape of the cask. Kepler could not help contrasting this crude technique with the more refined procedure followed in the Rhineland, where the volume was calculated from a combination of measurements or even obtained by counting the number of standard measures of fluid required to fill up the cask. The art of gauging was, in fact, a speciality of the Germans; they had written the standard textbooks on the subject. The astronomer was thus brought to reflect on the general problem of determining the volume of solids having the sort of all-round symmetry that a barrel possesses, what are called 'solids of revolution' because they can be formed in the way that a semicircle revolving about its base sweeps out a sphere in space.

This was the starting-point for Kepler's treatise on the *stereometry* or gauging of wine-casks (*Nova Stereometria doliorum vinariorum*, Linz, 1615). It grew out of a mere leaflet offered as a New Year's gift to two noble patrons. There were no printers at Linz; and it was in vain that Kepler's friend Marcus Welser tried to get the manuscript published at Augsburg: he was told that there would be no market for it particularly as it was written in Latin. Welser died in 1614; Kepler then recovered his manuscript, enlarged it beyond recognition and commissioned a printer newly settled at Linz to publish it. The book was on sale by the autumn of 1615.

The treatise is divided into three parts. In Part I, Kepler starts out from Archimedes and the mensuration of the circle, of cones and cylinders, conics and conoids, which enter largely into the contours of wine-casks, though he does not seek to match the rigour of the Syracusan's proofs. He conceives the circumference of a circle as made up of an infinity of infinitely short straight lines, and the area of a circle as made up of an infinity of triangles of which these lines are the bases. The ancients had usually avoided the use of infinitesimals because of the attendant logical difficulties. However, we soon pass into a wider field with the investigation of the volumes of solids of revolution, particularly those generated by a circle revolving about a line in its plane which either cuts, touches or does not cut or touch the circle.

An example is afforded by the 'anchor-ring', generated by a circle (EFD) revolving about an axis (AB) lying in its plane but not intersecting it (Fig. 10). This solid can be regarded as divided into an infinite number of disks by planes containing

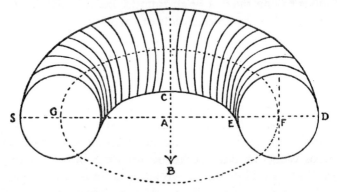

10. Finding the Volume of an Anchor-Ring

the axis of revolution. These disks are not uniform in thickness; but the inequalities may be supposed to average out to make the volume of the ring equal to that of a cylinder having for its base the cross-section of the ring and for its height the circumference of the circle described by the centre of the generating circle as it rotates round the axis. Kepler gave to several of the other types of solids generated in this fashion the names of fruits ('apple', 'gourd' and so forth) that they somewhat resembled; but this terminology has not survived.

Kepler next attacks what is really his main objective, the investigation of the solids (numbering over ninety) generated by the revolution of conics about exterior lines, or about tangents, chords or diameters, as axes. His aim was to employ these solids to approximate to the form of a cask in a way admitting of calculating the volume of the latter. Returning to one of the themes of his optical treatise of 1604, he remarks upon the continuity of geometric forms as exemplified in the way we can pass in an unbroken transition from the circle through the ellipse and parabola to the hyperbola.

Part II of the 'Stereometry' investigates the procedure appropriate to gauging the Austrian type of cask, whose two halves approximated to truncated cones. Kepler found himself asking what form a cask must assume in order for it to hold as much as possible in proportion to the quantity of wood employed in its construction, a condition that the Austrian cask came near to satisfying. He was drawn on to make a more extensive study of such so-called 'variational' problems; and he grasped the principle that a variable quantity remains fairly stationary in value as it passes through the neighbourhood of a maximum or minimum. In conclusion, Part III discusses the correct use of the gauging-rod for ascertaining the volume of casks.

A year later, Kepler brought out a freely adapted German version of his 'Stereometry'. The treatment is more popular and the material is better arranged; a useful addition was the attempt to systematize current tables of weights, measures and coinage. Kepler also included a glossary giving the German equivalents of Latin technical terms; it served to introduce *Kegelschnitt* as the German word for 'conic section'.

Kepler was obsessed by the cosmic significance of geometry, and he entertained something of a prejudice against algebra, notwithstanding the forward strides it had recently made; hence he did not allow algebraic methods to play the useful part they might have done in his stereometric investigations. And when Archimedean methods were inapplicable, he relied upon considerations of symmetry and analogy which occasionally led him astray. However, by breaking out from the bounds set to stereometry, Kepler rejuvenated the subject and powerfully stimulated the interest of his younger contemporaries.

CHAPTER SEVENTEEN

THE WITCH TRIAL

In Kepler's day the mind of Christendom was clouded by an obsessive fear of witches. Belief in witchcraft is an ancient and world-wide superstition not yet extinct; but it flared up with a terrifying emotional intensity as the Middle Ages drew to their close. Following the Reformation upheaval, the contending Churches felt their doctrinal foundations threatened to a degree unknown for a thousand years and more. They grew more than ever alert to heresy; and any suspicion of witchcraft touched a sensitive nerve, for what could be more heretical than to enter into a league with the Devil, as the witches were accused of doing? However, the witch mania derived much of its virulence from less spiritual motivations. Prosecutions for witchcraft were commonly based upon information supplied by informers. Such tale-bearing was enjoined as a sacred duty; and penalties were threatened against those who withheld the intelligence sought by the inquisitors. The detailed charges and the identity of the complainants were not made known to the accused persons, who were pressed by the threat or application of torture, or encouraged by false promises of lenience, to confess their guilt. Hence, all too often, prosecutions for witchcraft were instituted from motives of private enmity or spite.

Kepler lived out his days in a society convulsed by wars of flagrant atrocity, scourged by new and frightful forms of disease and haunted by death's-head fantasies of the imminent end of the world. It would not be surprising if in such an overwrought community there should be found some who exhibited the paranormal phenomena of mediumship and multiple personality that are now the concern of psychical research. More commonly, in an age that neglected the specialized care of the elderly, advancing years brought the less attractive aspects of the human personality into promi- nence and produced senile disabilities which it has become the task of geriatric medicine to alleviate. Many old women ap- proximated to the type that even now, in outlying country districts, still attracts the label of 'witch'. Such a one was Katherine, mother of John Kepler; and her protracted trial on a charge of witchcraft was perhaps the sorest affliction that ever befell the much-tried astronomer. Frau Kepler was nearly seventy years of age; she was more than commonly vulnerable to the kind of charges now made against her, being evil- tempered and a busybody with an interest in outlandish things. She had become senile, and under the prolonged strain of the trial her personality disintegrated still further; but she never admitted her guilt, despite all threats, and it was her obstinacy that saved her in the end.

The affair seems to have grown out of mere back-yard bickering between neighbours, Katherine having raked up the dubious past of a former crony. Nowadays the affair might have ended in the police court; but in those times the prevail- ing state of 'jitters' about witches placed a terrible weapon in the hands of the defamed woman which she did not hesitate to use against her accuser. She soon found allies; and a tissue of stories of a conventional type was quickly woven. Frau Kepler had proffered her guests a noxious brew; she had tried to obtain her father's skull for a drinking-cup; she had 'wished' aches and pains on to passing strangers; she had mad-

dened cattle and ridden a calf to death; she had compassed the
deaths of children, and so forth. Serious trouble began in
August 1615 when, at the court-house at Leonberg, where
she lived, and in the presence of a magistrate, Luther Einhorn,
but quite irregularly, Frau Kepler was threatened with death
unless she incriminated herself by working a cure by sorcery
on a woman whom she was alleged to have bewitched.
Katherine sought legal redress for this outrage; she was supported by her craftsman son Christopher, and by her daughter
Margaret and clergyman son-in-law George Binder, who all
lived in the neighbourhood and felt their own reputations
almost equally assailed.

By the time the news of these proceedings reached Kepler
in far-off Linz, he, too, had become involved in the net of
accusations, a natural association of ideas connecting star-
gazing and astrology with all sorts of wizardry. Kepler in-
dignantly rejected the charges against his mother and himself
and demanded a report on the legal position to date; and this
had the effect of finally silencing any accusations against the
astronomer. However, in order to extricate himself from the
civil case pending, the magistrate Einhorn managed to trump
up a further charge of witchcraft, involving a young girl,
against Frau Kepler, who now found herself in the situation
of a defendant, her own suit having been quashed, and who
committed the tactical blunder of trying to bribe the magistrate. She was persuaded to betake herself to her son at Linz,
where she was outside the jurisdiction of the court. For some
reason difficult to divine, perhaps through home-sickness for
familiar scenes, Katherine Kepler returned to Württemberg
in October 1617; her son followed to arrange for her legal
defence. The witch trial started in 1618 and dragged on until
the autumn of 1621, culminating in the examination of the
accused woman in the presence of the instruments of torture,

though she was not actually tortured. By her refusal to confess, and through Kepler's influence with the Duke and his advisers, Katherine Kepler regained her liberty on the family paying certain costs; she died the following year.

Meanwhile, in May 1618, the Bohemian rebellion had broken out that was to usher in the Thirty Years' War. Within a year the Emperor Matthias died; he was succeeded by the Catholic Archduke Ferdinand, under whom Kepler had fared so badly at Graz. His position had once again become precarious. In this crisis he was invited to settle in England by Sir Henry Wotton, the ambassador at the Imperial Court. Kepler felt a great admiration for King James I, to whom he had presented a copy of his book on the 'new star'; perhaps he would have done well to have accepted the invitation. Had he done so, he might well have lived longer and produced more. However, he felt too firmly bound by ties of loyalty to his German homeland; and he shrank from the physical restrictions of island life. And although many of Kepler's Protestant friends fared badly, he himself enjoyed the favour of the new Emperor, Ferdinand II, who confirmed him in his appointment as Imperial Mathematician. Kepler was undoubtedly sincere in the theological line that he adopted, but his dispute with the Lutheran authorities may have helped to soften the Catholic Emperor's attitude towards him and to shield him from much persecution. Indeed, the Catholics treated him with marked moderation throughout this period in the hope that he would eventually enter their fold.

Kepler had never accepted as final the refusal of the Stuttgart consistory to admit him to communion; he declared his intention of bringing the matter up again. He took soundings while he was detained in Württemberg by the witch trial; and in 1617 he addressed a direct personal appeal to his old teacher Matthias Hafenreffer, who had now become Chancellor at Tübingen, begging that his exclusion from communion might be rescinded. He hoped that the theological faculty at Tübingen might be induced to exert its influence in his behalf upon the consistory, with whom the decision of the case ultimately rested. Hafenreffer had long shown a warm affection for Kepler, to whom he had given wise counsel on the publication of his *Cosmographic Mystery* some twenty years before. He now found himself in a painful situation since he could not deny that Kepler's theological position was inconsistent with the Formula of Concord. After a brief correspondence with the astronomer, he laid the controversy before the faculty, and the final statement on the matter was signed by all its members: it finally dashed all Kepler's hopes of relief from that quarter, bidding him either conform or be separated from the Church as a man of reprobate mind. All that Kepler could do was to set down his convictions in a little tract printed for circulation among his friends.

CHAPTER EIGHTEEN

THE *HARMONY OF THE UNIVERSE*

Expulsion from his loved Church, the hideous witch trial of his mother, the deaths of his infant children, impending war all failed to sterilize the creative impulse in Kepler or to check his output of significant and highly technical writing. His long-term aim was the production of a set of planetary tables based upon Tycho Brahe's observations and the laws of the elliptic orbit. But under the stress of the middle years at Linz he turned aside to put into effect a youthful plan for writing a book on the Harmony of the Universe.

In his *New Astronomy* of 1609, Kepler had established once for all the precise shape of a planet's orbit and the simple law of areas underlying the apparently complicated variations in its speed. At a more speculative level, he had offered a broad physical explanation of the characteristics of a planet's motion agreeing well enough with the ideas of his time. But these developments involved only individual planets; they did not carry Kepler any further in his quest for some structural scheme embracing *all* the planetary orbits or some relation connecting the speed or period of a planet with its distance from the central Sun. In fact, his earlier hopes had been dashed by the discovery that Tycho Brahe's accurate observations agreed no better than the crude Copernican ones with his cherished hypothesis of regular solids interwoven with planetary spheres. Yet the measure of agreement shown convinced

him that there must be *something* in his reading of the cosmographic mystery; only the Creator must have had other considerations also in mind besides purely geometrical ones. So
Kepler toiled on through the years in the hope of some day
unveiling the ultimate reason why the structure and dimensions of the solar system are as we find them and not otherwise.

Kepler's earliest planetary synthesis was a purely geometrical one, involving no considerations of time. But surely time
must enter into the specification of a system of planets moving
at variable speeds and distances from the Sun. The cosmic
order must be manifested not only in symmetry but also, and
chiefly, in a harmonious interplay of elements in time, of
which music is the illustration that comes most readily to
mind. So the idea of a *harmony* in the Universe grew upon
Kepler as his hopes of establishing a purely geometrical order
faded; and this idea formed the germ of the most characteristic, and the most abstruse, of all his written works—the
Harmony of the Universe (Linz, 1619). The book, then, is about
harmony in a broad sense, and only incidentally about music;
still, it marked a notable advance upon earlier treatments of
the theory of music and it employed the musical terminology
and notation of the age. It was during the difficult period of
his early married life at Graz (about 1599, in fact) that Kepler
had planned and partly written this book. He was now to
carry it to completion with the deeper insight born of years
of discovery and reflection.

Kepler conceived harmony as a relation apprehended by a
mind without whose activity the harmony would not exist.
Ever since Greek times musicians had studied the sensations
produced by sounding two different notes simultaneously,
and they had distinguished pleasurable from unpleasurable
combinations, concords from discords. The number of ac-

cepted concords had gradually increased as the centuries passed, and Kepler recognized seven of them: the octave, the major and minor sixths, the fifth, the fourth, the major and minor thirds. He was anxious to discover just what it was that distinguished these from all other combinations of notes. The Pythagoreans and their successors had directed attention to the simple *numerical* relations connecting the length of a stretched string with the lengths of its segments vibrating in this or that concord with the fundamental note. Kepler, how-ever, insisted that the relation was a *geometrical* one; and he sought to establish a correspondence between the division of a vibrating string into equal segments and the division of a circle into equal arcs. One can imagine the vibrating string bent round into a circle and the segments becoming the equal arcs marked off by the vertices of a regular polygon inscribed in the circle. In elementary geometry we learn to distinguish between those polygons, such as the square and the hexagon, that can be inscribed in a circle by a ruler-and-compass con-struction, and those, such as the (seven-sided) heptagon, that cannot be so inscribed. There are, indeed, an infinite number of 'constructible' polygons; but Kepler, by imposing some rather arbitrary restrictions, managed to disqualify all of them except seven, which corresponded to his seven concords: 'the constructible in geometry is the harmonious in music.'

Now the construction of a regular polygon represents the solution of some algebraic equation; and when the construc-tion can be effected with ruler and compasses the correspond-ing equation is a simple or a quadratic one, involving either the first power or the square of an unknown quantity. Even so, the side of such a polygon, when expressed in terms of the radius of the circumscribing circle, is irrational; on the other hand, the equations of higher degrees corresponding to several of the non-constructible polygons, were known in Kepler's day; and their roots could be obtained to any desired degree of approximation. Hence it appeared to some mathematicians of the period that the distinction between constructible and non-constructible polygons was losing its significance. In extreme opposition to this view, Kepler regarded the constructible polygons as alone 'knowable', even to God, the others being just non-existent.

Kepler devotes most of the first Book of his 'Harmony' to ordering the constructible polygons according to the various kinds of irrational quantities involved, as these are classified in the tenth Book of Euclid's *Elements*. His second Book deals with what he calls the *congruence* of certain regular polygons (the square, the equilateral triangle and the hexagon), by which is meant their property of fitting together so as completely to cover an area with no overlapping and no uncovered gaps. Besides this *plane* congruence there is a *space* congruence where the polygons join up to enclose completely a region of space, thus forming one of the regular solids. There is also a brief note on *solid* congruence, the complete filling of space by a honeycomb of cubes or (less regularly) of rhombic dodecahedra. In the course of these investigations, Kepler discovered two of the so-called 'star polyhedra'. These were re-discovered about 1810 by Louis Poinsot, together with the two reciprocal forms; the complete set of four have come to be known as the Kepler-Poinsot solids.

In Book III Kepler shows how to construct the major and the minor scales, and he draws up rules for musical composition. Our enjoyment of music, he maintains, is not to be explained merely in terms of a pleasurable stimulation of the sense of hearing: 'The souls of men rejoice in those very proportions that God employed [in the Creation], wherever they find them, whether by pure reflection, or by the intervention of the senses in matters subject to the senses, or (without the exercise of reason) by an occult, innate instinct.' Music reveals to us an order which is the principle also of our own being; and it becomes the task of the astronomer to match the harmony without against the harmony within. Mathematical truths are not found but discovered, not manufactured but produced. Mathematical knowledge is self-knowledge. Plato had sought to explain our capacity for recognizing specific qualities in the world of experience, and our certainty about mathematical truths, by supposing that we could return in reminiscence to some previous state of existence in which we had enjoyed direct access to the realm of the Ideas. But Kepler held rather that God, when He fashioned man in His own image, necessarily implanted in his consciousness the fundamental harmonies that had served the Divine wisdom as a pattern for the creation of the world of nature. 'Geometry, co-eternal with the Divine thought before all things began (indeed, it *is* God Himself, for what is in God that is not God?), furnished God with models for fashioning the world and passed over into man with the Divine image: he did not receive it through the eyes.' In an appendix to Book III Kepler seeks evidence of harmony in the political sphere as manifested in the balanced laws of a healthy community.

In Book IV (from which the passage last quoted is taken) Kepler applies his theory of harmony to astrology which, as we have seen, attached much significance to *aspects*, or situations of any two planets with respect to each other. He supposed that the influence of such a combination would be most efficacious when the planetary pair subtended at the Earth an angle equal to that subtended at the centre of a circle by a side of one of his 'constructible' polygons; and he distinguished seven aspects answering to the seven musical consonances. However, after comparing his weather observations with the planetary indications over twenty years, he concluded that aspects corresponding to his so-called 'congruent' polygons possessed the greatest efficacy in calling forth storms and tempests.

Gathering up his scattered teachings on the economy of man's sublunary abode under the régime of the planets, Kepler conceives the Earth as an animated being. He presses fanciful analogies between its surface processes and the functions of a living body, likening the tides to the breathing of fishes. But how the soul of the body perceives significant planetary aspects (not to mention 'new stars' and comets) remains a mystery, though no more so than the process by which the image on the retina enters our consciousness. Our human apprehension of harmony may be merely instinctive, as when children or rustics respond to music. And at some such level of awareness (Kepler would have us believe) the soul of the Earth is alive to the celestial influences: 'The aspects sing forth; sublunary nature dances to the measure of the tune.'

In the fifth Book of the 'Harmony', Kepler forsakes man and Earth for the heavens. Rejecting the time-honoured Pythagorean doctrine, he maintains that it is the *speeds* and not the *distances* of the planets from the common centre of revolution that determine the celestial harmony. Now the speed of a planet helps to determine its period of revolution round the Sun; and these studies raised again in Kepler's mind the problem of finding a mathematical relation between a planet's speed, or its period of revolution, and its distance from the Sun. And it was after long reflection and in reliance upon the accurate planetary distances furnished by Tycho Brahe's observations, that, on 15 May 1618, he grasped (precisely how, we are not told) the vital relation that has come to be known as Kepler's third Law of planetary motion: the squares of the periods of revolution of the planets are to one another as the cubes of their mean distances from the Sun (the major semi-axes of their elliptic orbits).

Kepler, as we have seen, made the celestial harmony depend upon the orbital speeds of the planets; and with each planet he associated a note, not an audible one but a term in a mathematically determined relation. (But 'fill the heavens with air and in very truth music will sound forth', as he had written to Mästlin in 1599.) This note is determined by the angle that the planet would appear to describe in one day as estimated by an observer located on the Sun. These angular velocities were severally divided by arbitrary powers of two so as to reduce them to the same order of magnitude and to bring the corresponding notes all within the compass of a single octave. The ratio between any two of these angular velocities, so reduced, determined the musical interval between the corresponding notes and indicated whether that interval represented one of the seven accepted concords. As a planet described its orbit, its speed fluctuated, and the associated note accordingly rose and fell through a certain musical interval, being lowest when the planet was farthest from the Sun and moving at its minimum speed, and highest when it was nearest to the Sun. In fact, each planet performed a short musical scale, set down by Kepler in staff notation. The length of the scale depended upon the eccentricity of the orbit; and its limiting notes could generally be shown to form a concord (except for Venus and the Earth with their nearly circular orbits, whose scales were of very constricted range). Such concords might serve to explain why the eccentricities were as we find them and not otherwise. We need not follow Kepler in his discussion of the consonance between the notes emitted by neighbouring planets or of the harmonious anthem rendered by all the planets together at rare intervals, possibly only at the Creation, when complete concord prevailed and the morning stars sang together. Perhaps the age of the Universe might be estimated by reckoning back to the date at which that happy state of things must have prevailed. Such was Kepler's vision of the realm of nature. If we find it too demanding, we may prefer to picture his Universe in the homelier similitude of an old-fashioned clock, designed to keep strict account of time and season but also to delight the eye with its beauty and to charm the ear with its harmonious chimes.

In all earthly music Kepler sees an imitation of the heavenly. Singing in harmony (an art unknown to the ancients) man contracts all time into a brief hour and feels something of the Creator's joy in His finished work. Kepler, too, exulted in the revelation that he felt he had been singled out to receive: 'Behold, the die is cast; I have written my book, whether it be read by this generation or by posterity matters not; it may well wait a century for a reader when God Himself has waited six thousand years for a witness.'

CHAPTER NINETEEN

THE *EPITOME OF COPERNICAN ASTRONOMY*

Before we take up again the now shortening thread of Kepler's life-story, we must look at another of his major works dating from the Linz period. His *New Astronomy* of 1609 makes greater technical demands upon the modern student than perhaps any other of the historic books on planetary theory. Even in its own day it must have circulated almost exclusively among the mathematically accomplished. So, as was to be expected, Kepler was pressed by his friends to present the substance of the book to wider circles in the form of a manual of Copernican astronomy suited to the use of schools and designed to compete with the fashionable textbooks based upon the Ptolemaic doctrine. The fulfilment of this task was delayed in consequence of Kepler's private misfortunes and of his excursions into optics; and nearly ten years elapsed before he was able to publish, in 1618, the first part of his *Epitome of Copernican Astronomy*. A second instalment appeared in 1620; and the publication was completed in 1621.

Kepler could hardly have been encouraged to press on with the enterprise by the ban that the Roman Inquisition placed upon the first part of the 'Epitome', condemned for its Copernican teaching under the Edict originally directed against

Galileo in 1616. And many of the later, more theoretical chapters of the work had to be written or revised in the course of the arduous journeys that the astronomer was compelled to undertake in the defence of his accused mother. One consequence of the piecemeal composition of the treatise was that Book IV appeared with a different title from the rest and could be bought separately.

The 'Epitome' surveys the whole field of astronomical knowledge within the wider limits set by Kepler's own discoveries, and it presents his considered judgement on all the problems that were exercising the astronomers of his day. Whereas the *New Astronomy* had traced the devious route by which Kepler had arrived at his planetary laws, the 'Epitome' seeks a physical mechanism to account for them, and it explains how to apply them in practical calculations. Following the current fashion in school textbooks, Kepler gave his manual the form of a catechism of questions and answers.

Of the seven Books into which the work is divided, the first three deal mainly with matters that even today have not been developed much beyond the point to which the Greek astronomers carried them. They cover the geometry of the sphere and define the various circles ideally inscribed on the heavens and the Earth as aids to the description of the basic celestial phenomena. Kepler had been well grounded in this 'spherical astronomy' by Mästlin; he had learnt the latest improvements in the relevant methods of calculation from Tycho Brahe. However, at several points he went beyond the accepted limits of the subject, treating atmospheric refraction on the lines already familiar to us from his optical works. He estimates the height at which the atmosphere (conceived as of uniform density throughout) terminates as barely higher than the mountains; beyond that, space is filled only with the weightless aether.

Of particular interest is the appearance of Copernican teaching in the midst of all this conventional bookwork. Aristotle had maintained that heavy bodies seek the centre of the Universe and that the Earth is a concretion of such bodies. But Kepler held that a heavy body falls, not towards the centre of the Universe as such (for that is a mere mathematical point with no physical efficacy of its own) but towards the centre of another heavy body in whose sphere of attraction it finds itself. If isolated from other bodies it would have no weight, but it would still possess 'inertia' which, as Kepler uses the term, means a resistance to being set in motion by the application of an outside force and a tendency to come to rest when that force ceases to operate.

However, Kepler's arguments are chiefly arrayed in support of the hypothesis that the daily rising and setting of the heavenly bodies was due to a daily rotation of the Earth on its axis; and a few samples of his arguments may be of interest. Nature (he maintains) employs the simplest means; and she would not choose to set the whole external Universe in motion when she can accomplish the same end merely by a rotation of the inconsiderable Earth, which Kepler likened to a child's top set spinning. Rather than give a planet *two* motions, it is more reasonable to assign to each planet the motion peculiar to itself and to refer to the Earth alone the motion common to them all. Again, how *could* the whole external Universe revolve and the Earth stand still? If the Universe were *infinite*, how could the outer portions complete their daily circuit in twenty-four hours without travelling at an infinite speed (a possibility traditionally excluded for moving bodies)? But if the Universe is *finite*, it cannot move for there is nothing outside it to which its motion can be referred. 'Where nothing is at rest, there can be no motion.' Even in a finite universe, revolving daily, the speeds of the outlying stars would be incredibly high, contrary to the rule that, the larger an object, the slower it tends to move.

Kepler believed that a certain apparent inequality in the Moon's motion could be explained by supposing the length of our day to fluctuate slightly in the course of a year, being less in winter (when the Earth is nearer the Sun) than in summer. This made sense if the day were defined by a motion of the *Earth*, depending in some way upon the Sun's agency, but was inexplicable if the days were measured out by a revolution of the celestial vault. Again, the Earth's rotation has as its 'final cause' (its purpose) the fair sharing-out of the Sun's heat over the Earth's surface; but this is of concern to the Earth only, and the whole Universe cannot be expected to revolve in order to provide for it, as if a stupid cook should make the fire revolve round the joint on the spit! Kepler sees further evidence for the Earth's rotation in the westward ocean current alleged to be encountered by mariners. Moreover, heaven and Earth alike are material and can be kept moving only by some motive agency (natural or animal); and this can be more readily conceived as implanted in the solid Earth than as diffused through empty space. Again, the daily rotation, whether of the Earth or of the heavens, takes place about an axis fixed in the Earth (or so Kepler supposed) but moving about in relation to the stars (as is evident from the precession of the equinoxes). Hence the axis, and therefore the rotation about it, would seem to belong to the Earth rather than to the stars. And more to the same effect.

Kepler deals, as well as his defective mechanical principles permit, with the stock mechanical arguments against the Earth's rotation. It was maintained that the range of a cannon should appear to be greater towards the west than towards the east, as in the former case the projectile discharged from the cannon and the Earth's surface are moving in opposite directions and the apparent range should be the *sum* of their respective displacements during the time of flight, while in the latter case the range is the *difference* of the two displacements. It was also argued that a stone thrown up into the air from the moving Earth should fall far to the west of its point of projection. Maintaining the opposite view, Kepler points out that the flight of an apple thrown from hand to hand on a moving ship is not affected by the motion of the ship. He also contests the arguments that clouds and birds would be overtaken by the rotating Earth in its eastward course and that objects near the equator would be hurled off into space. Of great interest, as anticipating vital discussions of the problem by Galileo, Hooke, Newton and others, is Kepler's attempt at constructing the curve followed by a body falling from a height as it would appear to an observer stationed outside the rotating Earth.

Early in his 'Epitome' Kepler discusses the relation of the stars to the solar system. Astronomers before his day had generally regarded the stars as being distributed over the surface of a huge sphere having the Earth (or, as Copernicus maintained, the Sun) at its centre. Giordano Bruno, indeed, had taught that the stars are suns, fully comparable to our Sun, each travelling freely through infinite space accompanied by its train of inhabited planets, so that (as some modern astronomers claim) the Universe would present the same general appearance wherever the observer was situated. But Kepler was entirely averse to this way of thinking. He thought the appearance of the night sky indicated that the stars were grouped round a huge, starless, spherical gulf of space at the centre of which the Sun and his family of planets occupied an absolutely unique situation. As to how the stars were arranged among themselves, their differences in brightness suggested, though they did not prove, that the stars were at various distances from us. In any case space must be finite, for there can only be a finite number of stars, at finite distances one from another and therefore occupying a finite portion of space. And space cannot extend beyond that region, for space is a place where bodies *are* (an infinite void would be a non-entity). Many considerations induced Kepler to believe that the outer boundary of space was also a sphere, the most regular and capacious solid of all.

The second instalment of Kepler's 'Epitome', comprising Book IV only, appeared, as we have seen, in 1620. Its pre-occupation with Celestial Physics was prominently indicated on the title-page. Many ideas familiar to us from Kepler's earlier writings are here presented in their definitive form. Behind the discussions of particular topics and problems, the reader is aware of Kepler's quest for a unitary scheme of nature from which all the numerical specifications he was at such pains to estimate would follow of necessity. He sought, as far as possible, to 'mechanize the world picture', in Dijksterhuis's phrase, but also to demarcate the limit at which mechanical causation gives place to the régime of purposive spiritual agencies. And above both the mechanical and the spiritual principles he placed the eternal 'archetypes', the patterns in the mind of God in conformity to which He framed the worlds and which He implanted, too, in human minds, so that we recognize them in the world around us and a science of nature is made possible for us.

Kepler's 'archetypes' provided something of a bridge between crude sense perceptions and the mental concepts that somehow seem to arise from these. They constituted a cosmic order distinct from the world of phenomena and yet objective and not depending upon our choice. We come to understand the world of nature by matching external objects and processes against archetypal images pre-existent in our own minds. Wolfgang Pauli has drawn attention to the points of resemblance between Kepler's ideas and those of the psychologist C. G. Jung, whose writings have given to the terms 'archetype', 'archetypal', a new currency among students of these problems.[1]

Book IV of the 'Epitome' opens with a critical appraisal of Copernican astronomy, indicating how far Kepler judged the original scheme to need amendment in the light of deeper physical insights. The rest of the volume is divided into three parts treating respectively of the structure of the Universe, the planetary motions, and the inequalities (non-uniformities) in these motions. The fancied correspondence of macrocosm to microcosm is recalled when Kepler rehearses the arguments for the central position of the Sun, comparing the various physical agencies—heat, light, motion and the rest—to the several kinds of 'soul' that Aristotle attributed to plants, to animals, to rational man, and when he likens the Sun to the heart of the living body. The doctrine of the five regular solids in their supposed relation to the six planetary spheres finds its place here, together with equally groundless reasonings intended to relate the sizes, densities and masses of the several planets to their respective distances from the Sun.

Kepler approaches the central problem of the mechanics of planetary motion by way of his lately discovered third Law connecting a planet's period of revolution with its mean distance from the Sun. What keeps a planet moving despite its natural disposition to remain at, or to return to, rest? Astronomers in the Ptolemaic tradition (and Copernicus himself must be numbered among these) aimed at a purely geometrical representation of the planetary motions and made no

---

[1] See W. Pauli, 'The Influence of Archetypal Ideas on the Scientific Theories of Kepler', in C. G. Jung, *The Interpretation of Nature and the Psyche*, London, 1958.

attempt to explain *how* the planets are carried round in their complicated orbits. But natural philosophers, following Aristotle, had tried to solve this physical problem by postulating a set of revolving crystalline spheres (actuated by some sort of Intelligence or angelic ministry) to which the planets were attached. During the Middle Ages the two traditions were occasionally combined when hypothetical material mechanisms were substituted for Ptolemy's geometrical schemes. But Tycho Brahe had exploded the traditional belief in solid celestial spheres when he established that the comets move through the heavenly spaces without apparently encountering any such obstacle. So Kepler was now confronted with the problem of explaining how a planet managed to find its way through pathless space along an elliptic orbit and back to its starting-point. He saw grave objections to locating a freely acting Intelligence on the planet: such an Intelligence would be sure to confer a uniform circular motion, contrary to what was observed. He preferred to invoke some external motive force (*vis motrix*); its seat could only be the Sun, to which, indeed, he was prepared to ascribe some sort of soul.

Kepler's 'souls' were not reflective beings endowed with reason and will but entities of a lower kind whose function it was merely to administer a uniform driving force to a cosmic body, the resulting motion depending upon the divinely appointed constitution of that body. He supposed that from the Sun there emanate rays not of light but having some of the properties of light; as the Sun rotates, these rays lay hold of the planets and carry them round. The actual propulsion of the planets by these rays is a purely mechanical process; and the period of revolution of a planet is determined jointly by the mass of the latter and by the force exerted by the Sun (which falls off with increase of distance from the luminary).

In order to explain why a planet alternately approaches and

recedes from the Sun (as is prescribed by its elliptic course), Kepler invokes the agency of magnetism, or of something analogous thereto: he had read all that was known about magnetism in William Gilbert's great book on the subject, published in 1600. He conceives the Sun as a rather peculiar magnet having one pole at its centre and the opposite kind of polarity distributed over its surface (Fig. 11). A planet is like a bundle of magnetic fibres, its opposite hemispheres constituting the opposite poles of a magnet, one attracted and the

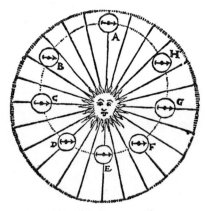

11. Kepler's Idea of the Sun's Action on a Planet

other repelled by the Sun. As the planet revolves round the Sun, its fibres preserve a fixed direction in space; each hemisphere is presented to the Sun in turn, and thus the planet is alternately attracted towards and repelled from the luminary; its resulting approach and recession condition an elliptic orbit. True, some planets, including the Earth, appear to rotate upon their axes in arbitrary periods; but this motion (Kepler supposed) affected only the *crust* of the planet: the magnetic *core* maintained a fixed direction in space.

Just as the Sun impels the planets, so these (though not self-luminous), by their rotations, carry round their own satellites;

and Kepler was able to verify that the moons of Jupiter conform to his third Law in their revolutions round their parent planet. Like the Sun, the planets are kept in axial rotation by indwelling spiritual principles; but their rotations are accelerated by the action of the Sun, so that the Earth, for example, makes 365¼ turns in a year instead of the ideal 360 turns. Thereby the Moon's rate of motion is also affected, so that there are more than the ideal twelve months in one year. As we are now aware, the Sun attracts both the Earth and the Moon as these two bodies revolve about their common centre of mass; but whichever of them happens to be nearer to the Sun suffers the more intense attraction, so that the Sun alternately pulls the Moon away from the Earth and pulls the Earth away from the Moon. Thereby an inequality, an alternate speeding-up and slowing-down, is introduced into the Moon's motion; it completes its cycle in about a fortnight and is called the *variation*. The further complication that the distance of the Earth-Moon system from the Sun fluctuates slightly in the course of the year introduces a further inequality: this is called the *annual equation*. Knowing nothing of such gravitational explanations, Tycho Brahe had yet detected these inequalities. And Kepler seems to have discovered the annual equation independently in 1598; he even tried to explain it to Herwart von Hohenburg in terms of competing forces emanating from the Sun and the Earth! Kepler, indeed, had the principle of Universal Gravitation almost within his grasp. His Sun was the centre of some sort of force varying inversely with distance; earthy bodies attracted one another within certain limits of distance. But he missed the full understanding of *inertia* as operating to resist change of motion as well as its inception.

Book V of the 'Epitome' serves to deduce Kepler's first and second Laws of planetary motion from the foregoing mechanical and magnetical presuppositions. Here occurs 'Kepler's Equation', fundamental in planetary theory but even now capable only of approximate solution in the process of calculating a planet's position in its orbit at a given instant. Since publishing his *New Astronomy*, Kepler had succeeded in showing, by a further recourse to Tycho Brahe's observations, that *all* the planets, and the Moon, conformed to the laws established in the first instance for Mars alone: this proved particularly difficult of accomplishment for Mercury, Venus and the Moon. So in Book VI he passes on to the problem of determining a planet's place as seen from the moving Earth, treating the latter just like any other planet. Methods of calculating eclipses, occultations and other such phenomena find a place here. The precession of the equinoxes and long-term changes are treated briefly in Book VII, which significantly hints at a correspondence between the behaviour of the rotating Earth and that of a spinning top.

All the endeavours of Kepler's earlier years had been an unconscious preparation for furnishing forth this *Epitome of Copernican Astronomy*. The title itself recalls that of his old master Mästlin's 'Epitome' from which in youth he had learnt the essentials of the science. True, the system set forth in Kepler's treatise could hardly be termed 'Copernican' any longer, for on the original basis of the Sun-centred planetary scheme he had erected a vast structure of celestial mechanics of which Copernicus had had no inkling. But Kepler seems to have been quite content that his own contributions should be regarded merely as aids to the understanding of Copernicus, whom he once likened to a priest celebrating at the high altar while he himself was content to serve as a door-keeper in the house of God.

CHAPTER TWENTY

FROM LINZ TO ULM;
THE *RUDOLPHINE TABLES*

With the 'Harmony' and the 'Epitome' safely published and the witch trial over, Kepler found
himself free to embark upon what was to be the
last major undertaking of his career: the completion and the
printing-off of the great set of astronomical tables which the
scientific world had long been awaiting with growing impatience. The work was to be entitled the *Rudolphine Tables*
because it had first been taken in hand under the patronage of
the Emperor Rudolph II. The underlying observations were
those of Tycho Brahe; but as Kepler's theoretical views gradually developed, it became inevitable that the tables should
be framed in accordance with his Laws of planetary motion.

In the accomplishment of his tedious task, Kepler was
forced to contend with obstructions of a kind that must by
now have become painfully familiar to him. Franz Tengnagel,
Tycho's jealous son-in-law, was no longer alive; but the surviving members of the family still grudged Kepler the use of
the dead astronomer's observations and they sought to place
restrictions upon his freedom to publish the Tables as he
thought best. However, the Emperor appointed referees to
adjudicate between the parties and, where necessary, to im-
pose a settlement. Again, Kepler encountered all the old diffi-

culties and evasions in his attempts to secure a grant to meet the cost of publication. He journeyed to Vienna and there sought to recover for this purpose some of the arrears of his salary going back to the days of the Emperor Rudolph. The Imperial government tried to honour these debts by drawing bills on provincial treasuries; but these claims were disallowed on various technical grounds. There was also the difficulty of finding a printer adequately equipped to set up the Tables and yet conveniently situated for Kepler to supervise the progress of the work. He would have liked to send the manuscript to Ulm; but the Emperor insisted that the book should be published in Austria, and preferably at Linz. So Kepler tried to build up the inefficient press there with types and workmen brought in from outside.

In 1625 violent measures were concerted against the Protestants of Linz; they were expelled under the threat of dire penalties. Once again, an exception was made in favour of Kepler; and this toleration was extended to the printer employed on his Tables. However, he became involved through regulations enforcing Catholic education on his children (he had his son safely smuggled away to Tübingen), and his library was impounded until his Jesuit friend, the mathematician Paul Guldin, came to his relief. The printing operations at Linz were brought to an end when the city was besieged by Austrian peasants in revolt against the Bavarian occupying forces. The press and the printed sheets were destroyed by fire; but Kepler's manuscript was fortunately preserved. After the relief of the city by Imperialist forces, he sought and received permission to transfer the work to Ulm; and late in 1626, with his wife, family and possessions, he bade farewell to Linz after fourteen years' residence there.

It had been Kepler's intention to sail up the Danube from Linz to Ulm; but when he reached Regensburg (also known as Ratisbon) the river froze over. So, having found a house for his family in that city, he resumed his journey in a wagon. At Ulm he took up his abode next door to an old friend now acting as the local medical officer. Kepler had always wanted his book to be printed at Ulm; he had even had some of the paper sent there though forced to make a start with the work at Linz. He had brought along with him the special lead types that would be needed. The printer at Ulm had been highly recommended; but Kepler came to believe that the man was imposing upon him. Following a dispute he resolved to transfer the printing to Tübingen; he set out in the depth of winter to walk to that city but was driven back by cold and fatigue. When at last, in September 1627, the printing was finished, Kepler's satisfaction was marred by a final protest from Tycho Brahe's heirs over the title and dedication of the work; and the opening pages had to be reprinted (twice indeed). Kepler took copies of his newly printed Tables to Frankfurt-on-the-Main in time for the autumn book fair of 1627; but the price could not be agreed upon with the Brahe family, and so the volumes could not be put on sale. They were first offered to the public in the spring of the following year.

Considering the fantastic circumstances under which the book was published, it is not surprising that the *Rudolphine Tables* should exhibit a somewhat conglomerate structure. The frontispiece (Plate IV) depicts the Temple of Astronomy supported on ten pillars, those directly presented to the reader each representing one of the great creators of the science, whose trophy it bears aloft. Kepler modestly occupies one of the carved faces of the base. He is seated at his study table, scribbling on the cloth as if too poor to buy writing-paper; but the Imperial Eagle is dropping him some coins. Following the stipulated statement by the heirs comes Kepler's narrative of the progress of the venture under successive Emperors. The introductory 'precepts' as to the use of the following tables begin with elementary arithmetic; worked examples show how to compute the precise angles and times involved in spherical astronomy and required to determine the positions of the planets, occultations, eclipses, corrections for refraction and other such quantities. There is a chronology of world history and a folding map of the world with a list of the longitudes of important cities reckoned from the meridian of Tycho Brahe's island observatory. The Danish astronomer's star catalogue is enlarged to include 1,000 star places; to these are added 136 more from the southern heavens, compiled by Kepler's assistant and future son-in-law, Jacob Bartsch. Kepler admitted that his Tables did not show exact agreement with the observed places of the planets even at the time of publication; and he warned astronomers that they would need revision as the years passed. Nevertheless, the *Rudolphine Tables* retained their pre-eminence for more than a century.

Kepler's lifelong endeavour to unveil the celestial mysteries involved him in a vast amount of tedious and time-consuming arithmetical computation. No man was better placed than he to appreciate the immense advance in the art of reckoning represented by the invention of logarithms, which serve to reduce multiplication and division to addition and subtraction, and the extraction of roots to simple division. The discovery came too late to be of very much service to Kepler personally; but one advantage of the long delay in the publication of the *Rudolphine Tables* was that it enabled sets of logarithms and instructions for their use to be included among the other aids to calculation.

The principal inventor of logarithms, John Napier, Scottish nobleman and divine, described his system in 1614; but his explanation of his method of calculating logarithms first appeared (posthumously) in 1619. Kepler caught a fleeting glimpse of the earlier book in 1617 while on a visit to Prague, but he missed its significance. Yet the underlying principle might not even then have been entirely new to him, since in his Prague days he had been in close touch with Jost Bürgi, the other reputed inventor of logarithms, whose system, though inferior to Napier's and not published until 1620, dated from that early period of Kepler's career. But the astronomer may not have gleaned much information from Bürgi, whom he later blamed for 'letting the new-born child perish instead of rearing it for the common good'. However, after studying Napier's explanatory supplement of 1619 at leisure, Kepler set himself to clear up the concept of a logarithm both as a mathematical entity and as an aid to calculation: these studies form the theme of his treatise of 1624 (with its supplement of the year following). Only after he had recast the theory and set it upon an arithmetical basis did he feel free to include a set of logarithms in his forthcoming *Rudolphine Tables*. Kepler declined to adopt the later improvements introduced into logarithmic technique by Napier and his friend Henry Briggs; his authority thus helped to keep alive for a time the original Napierian system. Neither Kepler nor any of the other pioneers in this field attained to the modern conception that the logarithm of a number x is an *index* showing the power to which a certain *base* must be raised to give the number x. Kepler sent his book on logarithms to Mästlin; but the old Tübingen professor was too set in his ways to see the importance of the invention, and it was eventually printed at Marburg by a well-disposed nobleman.

CHAPTER TWENTY-ONE

FROM ULM TO SAGAN

When Kepler returned, late in 1627, from the
Frankfurt book fair to his temporary abode at
Ulm, he had difficult decisions to make as to his
future domicile and means of livelihood. The Emperor's in-
tolerant religious policy made the problem seem the more
urgent. Kepler would have liked to be appointed as a lecturer
on his own Tables and on their application to the refined form
of astrology that he professed. He cherished the hope of printing Tycho Brahe's original observations upon which the
Rudolphine Tables were based. Meanwhile he returned to
Prague, whither the Emperor had lately transferred his court
for the coronation of his son as King of Bohemia.

At the moment the interminable war was going well for
the Emperor, who had summoned to the capital his victorious
commander-in-chief, Albrecht Wallenstein. Although a lone
Protestant in the now Catholic city, Kepler received from the
Emperor a welcome more cordial than he had hoped for,
together with the promise of a generous grant to cover the
cost of publishing the *Rudolphine Tables*. His fears of being
forced to give up his office of court mathematician were, for
the moment, lightened. However, he soon found himself
under renewed pressure to embrace the Catholic faith as the
necessary condition for his tenure of some desirable office to
which Ferdinand had it in mind to appoint him, and in which

he could have pursued his yet unfulfilled tasks. He thus became involved with Jesuit apologists, particularly with his well-wisher, the mathematician Paul Guldin. An exchange of letters between the two friends served to show the points at which Kepler's beliefs departed from the established Catholic doctrine and the reservations under which he would be prepared to take part in Catholic worship.

In a certain broad sense, Kepler held that the 'Catholic' Church embraced *all* baptized Christians, including Lutherans and Calvinists. That is the view still adopted by most Protestants, who claim to belong to a 'Holy Catholic Church' of which the 'Roman Catholics' form a branch, separated from their Protestant brethren by doctrinal differences, though the Roman Catholics of our day do not fully share this view. So Kepler deemed himself to have been a Catholic ever since his baptism in virtue of which he had since been guided into all truth through private study of the Scriptures and the creeds. The 'sinful divisions' (as they are now called) that separate the Churches arose, he maintained, from human error and frailty at the prompting of the devil. And while these divisions persisted, Kepler thought it best that the rival sects should co-exist peacefully side by side.

Kepler's visit to the Imperial court at Prague late in 1627 afforded him an opportunity of making contact with Wallenstein, then at the height of his power. And the stepping-up of religious pressure upon the astronomer seems to have set him wondering whether a brighter future might not be opened to him if he threw in his lot with the great military leader, who stood somewhat above the religious divisions of the age. The two men had already been brought into an odd sort of relationship through the interest they shared in what the stars foreshowed. Wallenstein's actions were governed and his decisions dictated by astrological considerations at the crude

popular level. In 1608 Kepler had received, through an inter-
mediary, a request to cast the horoscope of an unnamed
nobleman who was, in fact, none other than the youthful
Wallenstein, and he had complied on the understanding that
he should not be expected to furnish detailed predictions of
future events, as he did not conceive astrology as affording
information of that kind. The horoscope (Fig. 8, p. 84) has
been held to reflect accurately the character of Wallenstein as
it was to unfold itself on the stage of history; but there is some
reason to suppose that Kepler knew the identity of his subject,
which throws a rather different light on the episode. Subsequently, in 1624, the horoscope was returned to Kepler with
a request for a fuller elucidation as to certain specified con-
tingencies, and for an extension to cover future years. Kepler
once again refused to be pinned down to detailed predictions,
taking refuge in the commonsense consideration that events
depend very largely on the moral qualities of the participants
and not merely upon the stars or the other external circumstances: 'character is destiny', as we say. Peering cautiously
into the future, Kepler concluded his survey of Wallenstein's
unfolding fortunes within a month of the date of the great
leader's murder on 25 February 1634.

Wallenstein was thus already acquainted with Kepler and
well disposed towards him when they met at Prague in 1627.
In the course of his rise to power, the great soldier had become
a considerable landowner under the Emperor; and he had
recently received the Duchy of Sagan in Silesia as a fief. It was
soon arranged, with Ferdinand's approval, that Kepler should
be settled at Sagan at a generous salary and with a printing-
press for the publication of the works that he still had it in
mind to produce. In the spring of 1628 Kepler accepted this
appointment, albeit with some misgiving, for his fate would
now be bound up with the fortunes of his meteoric patron in

battle and at court. First, he visited his wife and children at Regensburg, where they had remained ever since the time of his migration to Ulm. Then he journeyed to Linz, where with all good will he was at last granted his release from the post of District Mathematician to Upper Austria. Lastly, having collected his family and such possessions as he needed, he repaired to Sagan, arriving there on 20 July 1628.

It soon became evident that Wallenstein expected from his protégé astrological briefing of a more superstitiously predictive kind than Kepler could honestly undertake to provide. However, the warrior arranged things to his own satisfaction by employing Kepler to calculate where precisely in the heavens the planets would be at the material times and then resorting to astrologers of the baser sort who applied to these data the conventional rules of their pseudo-science to divine what, at the personal or political level, the celestial concourse portended.

It also soon became painfully clear that the sorry pattern of Kepler's earlier years was to repeat itself at Sagan. The astronomer found himself in the position of a foreigner among his new neighbours, scarcely able to comprehend their speech and seeking in vain for any kindred spirit with whom to share his interests and designs. His loneliness was alleviated only by correspondence with scholars he had known personally in happier days. Most unfortunately, Kepler's arrival at Sagan coincided with a sudden application of pressure to force the predominantly Protestant population back into the Catholic fold. Even Wallenstein, who had always appeared indifferent to the religious issues of his time, deemed it to his advantage to promote this Catholic crusade. Once again the citizens were forced to comply with a régime organized by the Jesuits under threat of expulsion if they did not. Kepler was exempted from these requirements; but he was shunned by the townsmen, who feared to incriminate themselves by consorting with a misbeliever. One practical disadvantage for Kepler of the persecutions at Sagan was that he was unable to attract printers thither to help establish a press for the publication of Tycho Brahe's observations. It took months to collect together a press, printing operatives, suitable types and paper. Kepler found the task in view beyond him, so that astronomers had to wait until the present century to possess the Dane's observations in print: they occupy four volumes of his collected works. Instead, Kepler pressed on with his *Ephemerides*, almanacs of celestial phenomena and weather forecasts covering the years up to 1639.

Kepler was greatly assisted in the calculation of his *Ephemerides* by the young scholar Jacob Bartsch, whose interests lay principally in astronomy and medicine. He had first become acquainted with Bartsch at Ulm; and he came to form such a favourable impression of the young man's character and industry that he chose him to be the husband of his daughter Susanna, who had entered service in a noble household. Bartsch was induced to sue for the girl's hand in marriage, though he had never seen her; Susanna's consent was also obtained, and the wedding took place at Strasbourg in March 1630. Meanwhile, Kepler himself became a father again; his daughter Anna Maria was born in April of the same year.

CHAPTER TWENTY-TWO

KEPLER'S 'DREAM';
REGENSBURG; THE END OF
THE ROAD

At this late hour, Kepler brought to completion, and started to print, a curious astronomical fantasy that had slowly been taking shape in his mind over the years and to which he gave the title of *A Dream, or Astronomy of the Moon*. Already, in his *Conversation with the Sidereal Messenger*, addressed to Galileo in 1610, Kepler had announced that he had explored the possibility of landing on the Moon and had composed a 'lunar geography', or, more strictly, a 'selenography', to please his friend Wackher von Wackenfels. This work underwent successive revisions in the course of which it was turned into a piece of dream-legendry or science fiction to protect the writer from the consequences of identifying himself too obviously with Copernican ideas on the astronomical status of Earth and Moon. An early manuscript version of Kepler's 'Dream', originating from Prague in 1611, began to circulate widely; and Kepler believed that it reached and inspired the English poet John Donne. Eventually it arrived in Württemberg; and as it portrayed the dreamer's mother as an enchantress, it may have contributed to the prosecution of Kepler's own mother for witchcraft. His indignation at this misconstruction was expressed in the footnotes that he kept adding to his fantasy as the years passed, until the bulk of this commentary amounted to several times that of the text.

Several layers of allegory—personal, philosophic, political —have been discerned in the 'Dream'. But Kepler's primary purpose was to make the motion of the Earth appear more credible by demonstrating how an observer on the Moon (which everyone agreed was in motion) would inevitably, and quite adequately, interpret all the celestial appearances on the assumption that he was at the fixed centre of things. This idea went back to Kepler's Tübingen days. Kepler acknowledged some indebtedness to Plutarch, who had written on the 'Face in the Moon', and to Lucian, whose fanciful story of how he was carried to the Moon by a whirlwind had served the astronomer as a reading-book when he was learning Greek.

Kepler sets his dream in the year 1608, when his thoughts were running on the unnatural strife between the Hapsburg brothers Rudolph and Matthias. He had been watching the Moon and stars (he tells us) when he fell asleep and seemed to be reading a book he had bought in the book-mart. It told of one Duracotus of Iceland whose mother, the enchantress Fiolxhilde, lived by selling herbal charms to sailors. As punishment for some boyish prank, she sold him to a sea-captain, who left him in the care of the astronomer Tycho Brahe at his island observatory, where Duracotus spent several years learning astronomy. He then returned to his mother; and she called up a familiar spirit, a daemon from Levania, the Moon, who proceeds to voice Kepler's views about our satellite.

A voyage to the Moon, the daemon explains, is perilous and to be undertaken only by the hardiest, for our atmosphere extends barely to the tops of the mountains. The most acceptable space travellers are 'dried-up old crones who since childhood have ridden over great stretches of the Earth at night in tattered cloaks on goats or pitchforks'. To avoid being shrivelled up by the heat of the Sun, the traveller must wait for a lunar eclipse and then proceed along the axis of the cone of shadow cast by the Earth on the Moon. He must complete his journey during the four hours or so of the eclipse, so that the attraction of the Moon, the same as operates the tides, shall assist the ascent of the daemons who are bearing him on his upward way. A violent thrust is required to confer the necessary speed on the voyager; he should be previously drugged and the shock carefully distributed over his body lest he be dismembered. Provision must also be made against the airlessness and the intense cold of space. The Earth's attraction falls off with increasing distance until a point is reached at which the pulls of Earth and Moon are equal and opposite and force is needed only to overcome the 'inertia' (in the sense of sluggishness) of the traveller's body. Thereafter the Moon's pull predominates; and the problem is to ensure a 'soft landing', after which immediate shelter must be sought from the Sun's rays in underground caverns.

Moon-dwellers naturally conceive their globe as motionless. They behold the Earth as a globe fixed in space but *revolving* on its axis and measuring time for them, so that they might be imagined to call it *Volva*. The lunar globe is divided into two hemispheres: *Subvolva*, whose inhabitants always enjoy the sight of Volva and its phases, and the reflected light and warmth it sends them during their fifteen-day night, and *Privolva*, whose inhabitants, the Privolvans, are eternally *deprived* of the sight of Volva. Meanwhile, the sphere of the stars appears to revolve about the Moon in about twenty-seven days. There is little seasonal change for the Moon-dwellers; the zodiacal motions of the Sun and the planets are more complicated than those we observe; and what corresponds to the precession of the equinoxes proceeds much more rapidly. Kepler speculated about tides on the Moon, supposing it to have communicating oceans like the Earth. These tides will be highest when the Earth and the Sun appear in conjunction and their attractions are combined. He has something to say, also, about the strange creatures that inhabit the Moon, and about the circular, walled enclosures, still almost as mysterious to us as to Kepler.[1]

From this dream we return to the harsh realities of the astronomer's closing days. With the emergence of King Gustavus Adolphus of Sweden, the Thirty Years' War entered on a new phase; and it looked as if Sagan might soon be involved in the fighting. In the summer of 1630, at a crisis of the war, the Emperor summoned his Electors to Regensburg. They voiced the disfavour into which Wallenstein had fallen; and Ferdinand agreed to dismiss him. In the meantime Kepler had set out from Sagan for Linz in the hope of recovering some interest owed to him on certain bonds that he held there. On the way he called at Leipzig, at Nuremberg, and finally at Regensburg, where the great Electoral congress was still in session. He was preoccupied with the perennial problem of the huge debt owed to him by the Imperial treasury, and now, even more urgently, with the question of what his position would be following the fall of Wallenstein. Perhaps among the assembled princes some new patron might be found. Kepler had set out upon his journey in a hopeless mood, with no plans for returning to his family or for preparing some place to receive them. Upon reaching Regensburg, he took up his abode at a humble lodging in a street that now bears his name. After a few days he fell ill and soon became light-headed. The crude medical remedies of the time

[1] See *Kepler's Dream*, translated by Patricia F. Kirkwood, edited by John Lear, Berkeley and Los Angeles, 1965.

were applied to no purpose; local pastors hastened to offer spiritual consolations, but on 15 November 1630 John Kepler died, professing to the last his Christian hope and confidence. He was buried a few days later in the Protestant cemetery outside the walls of Regensburg; many of the princely company there assembled were at the grave-side. But when, several years later, the tide of war reached the city, the cemetery was destroyed; and soon all memory of the astronomer's last resting-place was effaced.

In their hour of need, the bereaved and penniless family found in Jacob Bartsch a faithful protector. He was anxious to complete the publication of the works that Kepler had in the press at the time of his death; but he soon learned that Wallenstein would meet no further printing-costs. Bartsch then resolved to press on with the production of Kepler's 'Dream' on his own account. When it became clear that Sagan would be overrun, the family fled to Lauban, Bartsch's home town. The curse of wandering descended now upon them as they fared to Prague, to Regensburg, to Linz, in their frantic efforts to secure some of the large sums owed to them. Eventually they returned to Lauban where Bartsch met his untimely death from plague. The astronomer's widow, after living for a time in Frankfurt-on-Main, returned to live at Regensburg until her own death in 1638. As some compensation for all the wealth of which his family had been defrauded, Kepler's son Louis, born of his first marriage, sold Tycho Brahe's original registers of observations to the King of Denmark. Kepler's manuscripts and collected letters followed a hazardous course into the hands of their modern editors. When Louis Kepler migrated to Königsberg in Prussia, he took this precious collection with him with the intention of publishing its contents. Upon his death, it was bought by the great astronomer Hevelius of Danzig and, after narrowly escaping destruction in the great fire that devastated his observatory, passed through a succession of hands until Leonhard Euler the mathematician persuaded the Russian Empress Catherine II to buy the collection, thus ensuring its preservation in Russia to our own day.

CHAPTER TWENTY-THREE

CONCLUSION

Before Kepler's achievements could be seen in all their significance, the great revolution in scientific ideas that he had done so much to set in motion had to progress much further towards its consummation. His permanently valuable contributions were embodied in his planetary Laws; and these were eventually to be fitted into a comprehensive scheme of natural knowledge within which they were to receive the type of satisfying physical explanation that he had long and vainly striven to provide for them. In the meantime, they severally rose or fell in the estimation of astronomers according to their acceptability to prevailing opinion or their applicability to problems in hand. At the same time, Kepler's historic planetary tables, founded upon the Laws, had to contend with the rival claims of other such aids to celestial prediction based upon the traditional hypothesis of circular motions for planets.[1]

The first Law (of the elliptic orbit), initially formulated for the planet Mars in 1609, was subsequently generalized to apply to the other planets and also to the Moon (neglecting specified disturbances that the Sun produces in our satellite's orbital motion). It was early employed as a calculating device in the construction of tables even by astronomers who incorporated it in a Tychonic planetary system, making the

---

[1] See J. L. Russell, 'Kepler's Laws of Planetary Motion: 1609–1666', *British Journal for the History of Science*, 1964, 2, 1–24.

planets revolve round the Sun, and the Sun round the Earth, in Keplerian ellipses.

It was the second Law (the one about areas described) that faced the hardest struggle to establish itself. This was partly because Kepler had originally formulated it in a somewhat ambiguous manner, hesitating between two only approximately equivalent ways of expressing it. Again, until the calculus was introduced, the second Law, as we know it, could not be elegantly stated in mathematical terms; indeed, to this day, it serves only approximately to fix a planet's position at a given time, using the leading terms of an infinite series laboriously derived from two other such series. It is not surprising that many seventeenth-century astronomers hesitated to accept such a geometrically inelegant proposition as embodying a fundamental law of planetary motion. Pythagorean criteria, or prejudices, as to the behaviour befitting a heavenly body still lived on.

Moreover, an attractive alternative to Kepler's second Law lay ready to hand. Where a planetary orbit is very nearly circular (as they mostly are) it fits the facts almost equally well (as Kepler was aware) to assume that the planet revolves at a uniform angular velocity about the *vacant* focus of its elliptic orbit (where the Sun is *not* situated). The French theorist Ismael Boulliau declared for this hypothesis in 1645: it was consonant with his conviction that the (perfectly elliptic) orbit of a planet was related to a *geometrical* order of nature and was not to be explained on *physical* considerations at all, and that the vacant focus of the ellipse must have some part to play. Within the wider class of Keplerian astronomers, Boulliau marked the emergence of a sub-group who accepted elliptic orbits but rejected all the physical scaffolding that had given verisimilitude to the area-law. To this school belonged Seth Ward, the Savilian Professor of Astronomy at Oxford, who introduced Robert Hooke to the science. However, Ward's colleague John Wallis, who held the Savilian Chair in Geometry, adhered to the area-law.

Kepler's third Law of planetary motion, initially relating the periods to the mean distances of the respective planets, was extended to cover the system constituted by the four satellites of Jupiter then known, in time for inclusion in Kepler's 'Epitome' of 1618–21. The work was widely read throughout Europe; and the Law seemed demonstrably true, though appearing to lack a theoretical *raison d'être*.

The propagation of Kepler's ideas owed much to the championship of the French mathematician Pierre Hérigone, the later volumes of whose massive textbook (1634–42) reflected his conversion to Copernicanism and his progress to a complete understanding of the three planetary Laws and their underlying conceptual mechanism. A disciple more celebrated, through the tragedy of his untimely death, was the young English astronomer Jeremiah Horrox. He became interested in Kepler's ideas after his friend William Crabtree had introduced him to the *Rudolphine Tables*, through which he was able to predict for 1639 a transit of Venus of which the two young men were the only spectators. Horrox went on to expound the celestial physics of Kepler (especially as applied to the Moon's motion) in a book that he did not live to complete and that first appeared more than thirty years after his death when the battle for the new astronomy was largely won. A convinced opponent of the Copernican theory, the Jesuit astronomer G. B. Riccioli, yet provided, in his *New Almagest* of 1651 (a belated counterblast to Galileo's 'Dialogue' of 1632), a fair and detailed account of Kepler's Laws. He also wrestled with the intractable problem of representing the path of an object falling from a height while sharing in the Earth's rotation. This problem went back at least to Kepler; it had proved too much for Galileo and it was soon to claim the attention and to tax the powers of Newton.

Galileo, the great Italian man of science, lived on for twelve years after Kepler's death; but to the end he remained un-appreciative of all that had been achieved by the genius of his German contemporary. Something mystical in Kepler's way of thinking, his reliance upon spirits, emanations, sympathies, proved incompatible with Galileo's positivist philosophy of nature. Even in his great defence of the Copernican theory, the 'Dialogue', published two years after Kepler's death, Galileo ignored the three Laws of planetary motion; and he made no acknowledgement to Kepler for all the arguments in support of the Earth's motion that he had thought out or given a wider currency. Another peculiarity of Galileo's 'Dialogue' was that it set the Copernican theory in its most crudely simplified form against the Ptolemaic, or even against the Aristotelian system, while ignoring the Tychonic scheme, which had by then become the only effective alternative to that of Copernicus. Galileo's appraising eye may have been impaired by some psychological 'blind spot' when directed to the achievements of Kepler; but we ought not on that account to minimize his investment in the emerging physical synthesis in which whatever was of lasting worth in Kepler's world-view was to find its place. Galileo's contribution to the re-formation of mechanics does not now appear quite so original or so definitive as it was formerly judged to be; yet his greatest achievements lay in this field.

Starting out from the traditional doctrines in which he had been schooled, Galileo early embraced the Copernican hypo-thesis, and he was led to consider how the Earth's motion could be related to mechanical principles, as he understood them. He had been taught that an earthy body would fall of itself towards the centre of the Universe (whether this was occupied by the Earth or not), while external compulsion would be required to make the body recede from that centre. But what of a body revolving *round* the centre? Would its motion continue of itself, or was force required to keep it moving? He saw the problem as analogous to that of a ball rolling down an inclined plane whose inclination to the horizontal was made vanishingly small. He was convinced that the ball would continue rolling for ever at a uniform speed, provided the 'plane' was really a huge spherical surface concentric with the Earth so that the ball was really revolving round the Earth. By the same token, it seemed natural to Galileo that, once the Creator had set the planets (including the Earth) revolving in circles round the Sun, they would continue to do so. He did not feel that any physical cause of such motion was called for; and that may partly explain his strange indifference to Kepler's efforts to exhibit the mechanism by which he supposed the planets to be kept revolving in accordance with his three Laws.

Whether Galileo ever advanced to the full doctrine of inertia, the perseverance of an undisturbed body in uniform rectilinear motion, is questionable. But his studies on the 'new science' of projectiles, published in his old age in 1638, related to motion over distances for which the curvature of the Earth was negligible. And they established the technique of determining a body's course by compounding its effectively rectilinear inertial motion with that imposed upon it by gravity. The law of inertia seems to have been first formulated in all its generality in 1644 by the French philosopher René Descartes, though only as an ideal law, for his universe admitted no void in which inertial motion could occur. He used the law to explain the illusion of a 'centrifugal force' affecting a rotating body. He conceived the planets as defunct stars revolving in a material vortex and kept in their orbits by the outward pressure of neighbouring vortices. And he explained terrestrial gravity as a reaction exerted upon gross bodies by more volatile particles revolving rapidly in a secondary vortex encompassing the Earth.

A momentous step was taken when a planet was first conceived as essentially a projectile. For its orbit could then be regarded as a trajectory from whose form could be deduced the law of the force keeping the body in that orbit. It was Robert Hooke, the inventive Curator of the Royal Society, who seems first to have grasped this conception and who pursued to the limit of his powers the problem of accounting for the motions of the planets on mechanical principles. Independently of Newton, Hooke universalized terrestrial gravity into a cosmic agency operating between all the bodies of the solar system and keeping the planets revolving in their closed orbits about the Sun. He sought to establish experimentally the law according to which gravity grew weaker with increase of distance from the attracting Earth. When he had correctly surmised the law to be that of the inverse square, he strove to explain the elliptic orbit of a planet as resulting from such a force directed to the Sun and imposed upon the planet's inertial motion. And though he failed in the attempt for lack of dynamical insight and mathematical expertise, yet it was Hooke who confronted his great contemporary Isaac Newton with the vital considerations that had to be combined to produce a convincing dynamical theory of the planetary motions. And it was Hooke's sense of the scientific importance of the matter, and his irritating persistence, that in the end overcame Newton's inertia and set in motion the great intellectual process that was to give us the *Principia*.

How Newton first became involved in the developing debate about the planetary motions is not known with certainty. According to the traditional account, based upon surviving memoranda in his own hand, it was as a Cambridge under-graduate, banished to his Lincolnshire home by the Plague of 1665–6, that Newton began to inquire whether the force of gravity might not extend to the Moon and perhaps help to keep the satellite in its course. Discovering for himself the rule that gives the acceleration in a circular orbit, he is sup-posed to have deduced, from Kepler's third Law, the inverse-square law for gravitational attraction, and to have applied it to find what the acceleration under gravity should be at the Moon's distance. Comparison of the result with the actual acceleration (deduced from the Moon's known distance and period of revolution) should have given fair agreement. New-ton's failure to press on with his investigation or to make a public announcement has been attributed either to a serious discrepancy in the results obtained, consequent upon his hav-ing adopted a crudely inaccurate value for the Earth's radius, or, more probably, to a mathematical scruple about reckoning distances from the Earth as if it were a massive particle con-centrated at its own centre. Some doubt, indeed, has been cast upon this traditional account by recently published manu-script material suggesting that Newton may have advanced more slowly than was previously supposed to his eventual mastery of the planetary problem; but this continues to be matter for debate.[1] It is not certain how early Newton ac-cepted Kepler's first and second Laws. There is evidence that, even as late as 1679, he allowed elliptic orbits as plausible but favoured the widely accepted hypothesis that a planet re-volved uniformly about a point displaced oppositely and equally to the Sun from the centre of the planet's orbit; in-

[1] See Derek T. Whiteside, 'Newton's Early Thoughts on Planetary Motion: A Fresh Look', *British Journal for the History of Science*, 1964, *2*, 117–37; J. W. Herivel, 'Newton's First Solution to the Problem of Kepler Motion', *ibid.*, 1965, *2*, 350–4.

and his Cambridge paper at Cambridge 1969 Summer meeting!

deed, he experimented with refined forms of this hypothesis.

However, it seems accepted that, in the winter of 1679–80, Newton (whatever he had accomplished previously) was moved to look more deeply into the planetary problem. The occasion for this was some correspondence he had with Robert Hooke, from whom he had become estranged following Hooke's lively criticisms of Newton's theory of colours. Replying to a friendly advance by Hooke, Newton mentioned somewhat casually that a body dropped as from a high tower upon the (eastward) rotating Earth would not appear to fall towards the *west*, as the old-time teachers of mechanics would have had it, nor would it appear to fall *vertically*, as Galileo would probably have maintained. The body would show an *eastward* deviation from the vertical; and Newton gave a sound reason for this. Hooke tried to demonstrate the phenomenon; his claim to have succeeded must have been mistaken. Newton and Hooke then became drawn into a discussion as to the path that would be followed by the falling body if it could continue its free fall below the Earth's surface without encountering any obstruction. At first Newton, failing to grasp the cosmic implications of the problem, assumed a uniform gravitational attraction all the way to the Earth's centre. However, Hooke came up with the inverse-square law (which he had arrived at somehow), though maintaining that, below ground, the attraction would fall off as the Earth's centre was approached, with more and more of the Earth's substance lying above the body and pulling it upward. Gravity was not something with which only the Earth's centre was concerned. Without waiting for a reply, Hooke pressed Newton to establish mathematically what curve would be described by a body under a force directed towards a fixed centre and varying inversely as the square of the distance therefrom. It did not take Newton long to prove (by a mathematical technique that only he knew how to employ) that the required curve was an ellipse (or, more generally, a conic) with the Sun in one focus. At the same time, he established that Kepler's Law of areas holds of *any* such 'central orbit', whatever the assumed law of force. So much for Kepler's first and second Laws. The third Law was already widely recognized as implied by the inverse-square law of attraction.

Newton laid his calculations by (indeed he lost them) until 1684, when he was recalled to the problem by his younger contemporary Edmond Halley, who voiced the growing impatience of the Royal Society mathematicians to read the elusive riddle of the planetary motions. Continuing his investigations at Halley's instance, Newton was able to prove with mathematical exactitude what he and Hooke had previously employed as a mere working-hypothesis, namely, that a body such as the Earth (a sphere supposed of uniform density throughout, or as composed of concentric shells each uniformly dense) attracts any external body, even if close to the Earth's surface, as if the Earth's mass were all concentrated at the Earth's centre. The establishment of this theorem conferred a new rigour upon Newton's hitherto tentative calculations; and he was emboldened to proceed with his synthesis, under his Laws of Motion and of Universal Gravitation, of a wide range of celestial and related phenomena—the orbital motions of the planets, the intricate course of the Moon, the vicissitudes of comets, the Earth's departure from an overall spherical form, the precession of the equinoxes, tides, even the discrepancies that soon became evident in Kepler's third Law itself. These applications form the essential content of Newton's *Principia*—the 'Mathematical Principles of Natural Philosophy'—which was completed in 1686 and published in the following year.

Thus Newton wove whatever was of enduring value in

CONCLUSION

Kepler's world-view into his own historic synthesis, destined to retain its authority unquestioned for some two hundred years and to set the pattern for a broadening web of physical theory extending into regions of experience that neither Kepler nor Newton had ever entered. Only in the present century have scientists felt compelled, on experimental evidence, to abandon the implicit assumption underlying so much of the bitter dissension we have had to chronicle in the foregoing pages—the assumption, namely, that a physically verifiable distinction can be drawn between bodies at rest and bodies in motion. So men of our own age have had to take up again the ancient quest for understanding of the natural world and to add fresh chapters to the story whose earlier course filled our opening pages.

Of that story there is no foreseeable end; in that quest no final goal is ever attained. Only it has been sometimes given to one or another to take a giant's stride forward along the endless road. Such a one was John Kepler. Led on by his Platonic dream of a celestial harmony, he sought and found mathematical regularities in nature such as we should not expect to find except at the ultimate atomic level, but which proved to be essential to the Newtonian revolution in celestial mechanics with all that has flowed from it. Had Newton never lived, it is probable that some men less gifted than he would have derived the whole gravitational theory of the planetary motions from ideas that were in the air at the time— the doctrine of inertia, Kepler's Laws, the infinitesimal technique. But if Kepler had not lived or had not enjoyed access to the recorded observations of Tycho Brahe, even Newton could not have made good that deficiency, and the whole subsequent development of European thought, the whole course of modern world history, would have been changed beyond conjecture.

GLOSSARY

Accommodation. The automatic adjustment of the eye to ensure distinct vision of objects at various distances.

Apses. The two points on a planet's orbit where it is respectively nearest to and farthest from the Sun or other central body.

Conic Sections. The curves formed by the intersections of a (right circular) cone with variously inclined planes.

Conjunction. A close approach of two or more planets to one another in the sky.

Ecliptic. The Sun's apparent annual path through the heavens.

Genethliac. Relating to the casting of horoscopes.

Horoscope. An astrological diagram of the heavens, indicating the configuration of the planets at a critical instant (e.g. the time of a child's birth).

Hyperboloidal. Having the form of the surface generated by the rotation of a hyperbola (one of the *conic sections*) about its axis.

Integration. A mathematical technique for summing the increments of a continuously varying quantity.

Irrational. Incapable of being expressed as the ratio of two positive whole numbers.

Kinematic. Relating purely to motion, without reference to force or mass.

Macrocosm and Microcosm. The 'great world' of the Universe and the 'little world' of the human frame, conceived as exhibiting a detailed mutual correspondence.

Occultation. The interposition of the Moon between the observer and some planet or star.

Parallax. The apparent shift in the position of an object consequent upon an actual displacement of the observer.

Precession of the Equinoxes. The return of the equinoxes before their due time, and the consequent shortening of the seasonal year, resulting from a slow conical motion of the Earth's axis in space; the word *precession* is applied also to this motion itself.

Retrogression (retrograde motion). An angular motion from east to west periodically interrupting a planet's normal eastward apparent course round the heavens.

Spherical Aberration. A defect of the image formed by an optical system composed of spherical reflecting or refracting surfaces.

Stereometry. The technique of estimating the volumes of solids.

Transit. The visible passage of the planets Venus or Mercury across the Sun's disk.

INDEX

Alexander the Great, 82
Apian, P., 27
Apollonius of Perga, 73
Archetypes, 16, 42, 157-8
Archimedes, 135
Aristotle, 16-18, 34, 38, 48, 54, 76, 82, 85, 153, 158-9
  his system of nature, 16-17, 37, 182
Astrology, 27, 29-30, 37, 81-6, 97-8, 102-6, 108-10, 127, 133, 148-9, 169-71
Atomists, 14

Bär, N. R. (Ursus), 56-7
Bartsch, J., 166, 172, 177
Binder, G., 141
Boulliau, I., 180
Brahe, Tycho, 39, 53-70, 74-5, 85, 87, 89, 91, 94-6, 99-100, 102, 104, 107, 109-111, 128, 144, 153, 159, 161-3, 166, 172, 174
  his planetary system, 39, 55-6, 64, 68, 179
Briggs, H.,167
Bruno, Giordano, 53, 101, 115, 156
Brunowski, J., 101
Bürgi, J., 66, 167

Calvin, J., 19
Caspar, M., 5-6

Catherine II, Empress, 178
Charles (Hapsburg), Archduke, 29
Chiaramonti, S., 110-11
Chronology, 131-3
Comets, 23, 28, 54, 94, 101, 105, 107-11, 149, 187
Conic Sections, 24, 91, 137, 189
Copernicus, N., 18, 28, 30, 37-8, 40, 52, 55, 67, 162
  his planetary system, 18, 28, 30, 37-9, 41-2, 52-3, 55-6, 64, 68, 105, 158, 182
Cosimo II, Grand Duke of Tuscany, 117-18
Cosmology,
  primitive, 13-14, 33
  Greek, 14-17, 33-4
  Medieval, 18
Crabtree, W., 181
Crystals, 126-7

Descartes, R., 90, 183-4
Dionysius Exiguus, 133
Donne, J., 173
Dyck, W. von, 6

Earth, 13, 15, 17-18, 28, 33-40, 42, 45-7, 55-6, 67, 70-2, 77-9, 86-7, 97, 99, 108-9, 149-50, 154-6, 160-2, 174-5, 182-6
  motions of, 18, 28, 37-9, 42, 52,

INDEX

Earth—*cont.*
    55–6, 67, 70–2, 109, 154–6, 160, 162, 182
Eclipses, 23, 29, 53, 63, 89, 93–6, 162, 175
Einhorn, L., 141
Epicycles, planetary, 35–7, 42, 67
Equants, planetary, 36, 50, 67, 69–72
Eriksen, J., 96
Ernst, Elector of Cologne, 120–1, 124
Euclid, 45, 134
Eudoxus of Cnidus, 17, 34
Euler, L., 178

Fabricius, J., 113
Ferdinand (Hapsburg), Archduke, Emperor, 29, 58, 63, 142, 163–4, 168, 170, 176
Feselius, P., 105–6
Frederick II, King of Denmark, 55, 66

Galilei, Galileo, 52–3, 93–4, 111, 113–22, 128, 153, 156, 173, 182–3, 186
Gassend, P., 113
Gilbert, W., 77, 160
Grassi, H., 111
Gravitation, Universal, 161, 184–8
Gravity, 52, 76–8, 181–2, 184–5
Gregory XIII, Pope, 131
Guiducci, M., 111
Guldenmann, M., 21
Guldin, P., 110–11, 164, 169
Gustavus, Adolphus, 176

Hafenreffer, M., 143
Halley, E., 107, 187
Harmony, 15, 39, 41–2, 145–51
Harriott, T., 114
Hellman, C. Doris, 6
Hérigone, P., 181
Hesiod, 13
Hevelius, J., 177–8

Hoffmann, J. F., Baron, 102
Hohenburg, Herwart von, 58, 132, 161
Homer, 13
Hooke, R., 156, 181, 184, 186
Horky, M., 118
Horrox, J., 181

Ibn al-Haitham (Alhazen), 88, 90, 92

James I, King of England, 142
Jesuits, 29, 52, 58, 61, 65, 110–11, 164, 169, 171
Josephus, 133
Jung, C. G., 158
Jupiter, 31–2, 42, 45, 54, 97–8, 101, 115, 120
    satellites of, 115, 117, 161

Kallwitz, S. (Calvisius), 133
Kepler, John (Johannes), *passim*
    at Tübingen, 26 ff.
    at Graz, 29 ff.
    at Prague, 63 ff.
    at Linz, 12 ff.
    at Ulm, 165 ff.
    at Sagan, 171 ff.
    at Regensburg, 176–7
Kepler, John,
    his *Cosmographic Mystery*, 41–52, 56, 67, 77–9, 115, 143
    his *New Astronomy*, 68–75, 77, 87, 115, 125, 144, 152–3
    his *Supplement to Witelo*, 72, 88–95, 110, 112
    his *New Star in Serpentarius*, 100–4
    his *Three Tracts on Comets*, 109–10
    his *Dioptrics*, 121–4
    his *Stereometry*, 134–7
    his *Harmony of the Universe*, 86, 145–51, 163
    his *Epitome of Copernican Astronomy*, 79, 152–63, 181

INDEX

Kepler, John—*cont.*
  his *Rudolphine Tables*, 64, 110, 129, 163–8, 181
Kepler, John, his Laws of planetary motion, 5, 62, 72, 74, 144, 149–50, 161, 179–82, 185–8
Kepler, Anna Maria (*daughter*), 172
Kepler, Barbara, *née* Müller (*first wife*), 57–8, 63–5, 127–8
Kepler, Christopher (*brother*), 22, 141
Kepler, Frederick (*son*), 66, 127
Kepler, Henry (*father*), 21–5
Kepler, Henry (*brother*), 22
Kepler, Henry (*son*), 58
Kepler, Katherine, *née* Guldenmann (*mother*), 21–5, 140–2, 153, 173
Kepler, Louis (*son*), 66, 130, 177
Kepler, Margaret (*sister*), 22, 141
Kepler, Regina (*step-daughter*), 57, 63, 66
Kepler, Susanna, *née* Reutinger (*second wife*), 129–30, 164, 171, 177
Kepler, Susanna (*daughter, first of the name*), 58
Kepler, Susanna (*daughter, second of the name*), 66, 172
Koestler, A., 6

Lange, E., 56
Leonardo da Vinci, 119
Leopold (Hapsburg), Bishop of Passau, 127
Light, properties of, 49, 87–93, 121–3
Logarithms, 66, 166–7
Longberg, C. (Longomontanus), 61
Lucian, 174
Luther, M., 19

Magnetism, 76–7, 160
Manilius, M., 82
Mars, 31–2, 37, 42, 45, 61, 66–70, 87, 97, 99–101, 115, 121, 162, 179

Mästlin, M., 27–8, 41, 47, 51–2, 54, 58, 60, 73, 94, 99, 101, 107, 109, 112–13, 119, 127, 150, 153, 162, 167
Matthias (Hapsburg), Archduke, Emperor, 121, 125, 127–8, 130, 142, 174
Maurolycus, F., 93
Mechanics, celestial, 5, 31, 48–50, 76–9, 154–61, 182–8
Melanchthon, P., 26
Mercury, 31–2, 42, 45, 48, 61–2, 112–13, 115, 120, 162
Moon, 17, 23, 27, 29, 31–2, 34, 39–40, 47, 54–5, 63, 78–9, 85–7, 89, 94–5, 99–100, 106–7, 111, 116–20, 132, 155, 161, 173–6, 179, 181, 185, 187
  motion of, 32, 34, 78, 95, 155, 161, 179, 181, 185, 187
Müller, J., 57, 64

Napier, J., 166–7
Newton, Sir I., 5, 132, 156, 182, 184–8

Parallax, 27, 38–9, 94–5, 99–101, 109, 190
Pauli, W., 158
Planets, 15, 17–18, 31–50, 54–6, 68–74, 82–6, 97–101, 113, 144, 149–50, 166, 187
  conjunctions of, 43, 54, 97, 189
  motions of, 17–18, 32, 34–6, 42, 55–6, 67–72, 113, 149–50, 166, 187
  number of, 41
  orbits of, 35–7, 41, 68–74, 144
  periods of, 32, 41, 43, 48, 50
Plato, 15–18, 34, 39, 41, 45, 50, 82
Plutarch, 94, 174
Poinsot, L., 147
Precession, 155, 162, 181, 190

INDEX

Ptolemy of Alexandria, 17–18, 36–8, 50, 83, 90, 159
  his planetary system, 17–18, 36–8, 41, 68, 182
Pythagoreans, 15–16, 33, 146, 180

Reformation, 19–20, 22, 83
Refraction, atmospheric, 87, 91, 153
  laws of, 88, 90–1, 121–2
Reuchlin, J., 26
Riccioli, G. B., 181
Rosen, E., 105, 119
Röslin, H., 104–6
Rudolph II, Emperor, 5, 58, 61, 64–5, 73–4, 99–100, 104, 112, 116, 125, 127–8, 163–4, 174

Saturn, 31–2, 43, 45, 48, 54, 97–8, 115, 121
Scaliger, J., 131
Scheiner, C., 113, 123
Scientific Revolution, 12, 52
Snell, W., 90
Socrates, 15
Solids, regular (Platonic), 15, 43–7, 60, 74
Space travel, 120, 173–5
Stadius, G., 28
Stars, 31–2, 38–9, 42, 117, 119–20, 166
  distribution of, 102, 156–7
Stars, 'new' (novae), 27, 54, 97–105, 107, 149
Stereometry, 134–8, 190

Sun, 14, 18, 31–3, 35, 37, 39–43, 45–50, 55–6, 67–72, 76, 79–80, 85–90, 93–6, 108, 112, 119–20, 145, 150, 156, 158–61
  rotation of, 79–80, 113, 159
Sunspots, 112–13
Suslyga, L., 132

Telescope, 'Galilean', 114–23
  'Keplerian', 123
Tengnagel, F., 74–5, 96, 163
Thirty Years' War, 5, 22, 109, 142, 176
Tides, 78, 149, 187

Venus, 31–2, 37, 42, 45, 94, 109, 115, 121, 162, 181
Vision, physiology of, 91–2, 123

Wackher von Wackenfels, M., 112, 115, 126, 173
Wallenstein, A., 84, 168–71, 176–77
Wallis, J., 181
Ward, S., 180–1
Welser, M., 135
William IV, Landgrave of Hesse, 54–5, 66
Witch mania, 139–40
Witelo (Vitellio), 88, 90–2
Wotton, Sir H., 142

Zwingli, H., 19